AN AMHERST BOYHOOD

An Amherst Boyhood

by

ALFRED E. STEARNS

Foreword by *Chief Justice* Harlan F. Stone

ONE HUNDRED TWENTY-FIFTH ANNIVERSARY

AMHERST · MASSACHUSETTS
PUBLISHED BY THE COLLEGE

COPYRIGHT, 1946, BY AMHERST COLLEGE

PRINTED IN THE UNITED STATES OF AMERICA
BY THE PLIMPTON PRESS · NORWOOD · MASS

Contents

Foreword

To KNOW A BOOK ONE MUST know its author. But my classmate Alfred E. Stearns, who has generously undertaken to prepare this volume as the means of sharing with others his cherished recollections of Amherst town and College, needs no introduction to an Amherst audience. In his case a foreword could add little to our knowledge of the author. At most it can serve only to revive our own recollections and, by adding them to his, add something, perhaps, to the picture of Amherst which he gives us.

Few graduates of Amherst have been so intimately associated with the town and College, or are so well qualified as the author to write this book of Amherst reminiscences. For more than the traditional three score years and ten " Al " Stearns has been as much a part of the Amherst scene as the Holyoke Range or the College church, which was donated to the College by his father, and its cornerstone laid the year before the birth of the son.

Al Stearns' grandfather, William A. Stearns, was the fourth President of the College, and a successful one, from 1854 until his death in 1876. After the death of the father, Al's mother took up her residence in Amherst, where she conducted, in what is now the President's house, the Stearns' School for Girls. It was known as " the Convent " to successive generations of Amherst students, who, as they passed to and from classrooms and chapel, seldom failed to cast furtive glances at the school and its fair occupants. From 1874 until his graduation from Amherst with the renowned Class of '94, Al Stearns made Amherst his home, and it has never since ceased to be the lodestone of his interest.

As a teacher at Phillips Andover Academy, and later as its distinguished headmaster for thirty years (1903–1933), he turned toward Amherst its quota of Andover boys, to fructify and strengthen the liberal tradition of the College. Since 1927 he has been a trustee of Amherst College. In 1937 he succeeded the late George A. Plimpton as Chairman of the Board of Trustees. To the duties of that office he has given unsparingly of his time and energy, and by his wise counsel and devotion to the College has contributed much to President King's successful administration.

In college days Al Stearns was among the most prominent and influential undergraduates. This was owing principally to his personality and character. But these were powerfully reinforced by his fame and popularity as an athlete, which were by no means confined to the Amherst campus. He was admired because of his skill and prowess on the baseball and football fields, and as a tennis champion, but he was also respected because of his good sportsmanship and love of fair play. Amherst men of his day will remember many a thrilling battle on the baseball field in which he played a decisive part. Those who witnessed the famous football game of 1891 between Amherst and Williams can never forget the fortitude and skill with which he, as Amherst's impromptu fullback, frustrated Williams' confident expectations of victory.

Amherst students who, like Al Stearns and myself, were also town boys, are the grassroots members of the Amherst brotherhood. We had the advantage of varied opportunities to gain youthful insight into the life and activities of the College community, which had for us a special significance. We knew better than those who came from urban communities to become adopted sons of the town for only four years, the beauty of its setting and all the attractions of its countryside. We swam in and skated and boated on the Freshman River. We roamed the surrounding hillsides in search of the first wild flowers of spring and of chestnuts and hickory nuts in the fall. We sought out the trout streams which nestle in the Pelham Hills and in the woods on the south side of Norwottuck. On occasion we fished at night in the ponds near Belchertown and Granby, and we visited Hop Brook, which, flowing from the southeast into the upper reaches of the Freshman, could, under favorable conditions and by suitable persuasion, be made to yield some speckled beauties to the creel. We knew and understood the people of the countryside and, knowing them, the pious devotion, with which in an earlier day the farmers of the Pelham Hills and of the Connecticut River Valley had brought gifts for the founding of the College, was to us no mystery.

In awe and admiration we worshipped from afar the gods of the College community. President Seelye readily fitted the part of Zeus in our mythology. " Old Doc," " Emmie," and " Old Ty," with their bearded countenances and dignified bearing, seemed to us like recent arrivals from Mount Olympus itself. Of more earthly character, and more approachable, or so we thought, were our student heroes of the athletic fields and of the College platform.

Al Stearns has drawn upon these and many other recollections of Amherst town and College life in portraying them for us. They will stir similar memories in others and in not a few of us nostalgic longings for those Amherst days which are gone, not to return, when with our first draughts from the Pierian spring we were stirred to seek knowledge of the epic which is life.

In lighter vein he tells us of " quaint " characters of the town who, on occasion, added to the gaiety of college days — and nights. He pays tribute, in which all Amherst men will join, to those members of the faculty who, through the years, have built their lives into the structure of the imponderable Amherst, to make it what it is. He reminds us of the debt which we owe to Garman, Morse, Harris, Frink, Olds, and " Billie " Cowles, and many another. He rightly finds the source of their enduring influence over us in the fact that beyond their intellectual qualities they had the gifts of the teacher or the subtle and undefinable power of distinguished personality.

To those of us who knew these men, their statures have not grown less through the years. They were great men to us then. The disillusionments of a half century out of college do not make them seem less so now. By these pages Al Stearns, himself a true product of Amherst College, makes his offering to his fellow Amherst men, of joyous recollections of the fortunate days we spent there. To the College he renders a service, when he reminds us that in the years to come we must ever look to the worthy successors of these men to strengthen and revitalize the power of Amherst College as a teacher of men. For both, Amherst College and her sons will be grateful.

HARLAN F. STONE

AN AMHERST BOYHOOD

I · *Early Years in a College Town*

THE TOWN OF AMHERST, Massachusetts, in the early years of the last quarter of the past century, was a quiet, self-contained, and friendly village. The New London Northern Railroad, connecting at Palmer with Boston and Albany trains to the east and west, and Paige's famous stagecoach, which daily covered the seven miles journey each way to Northampton and back, supplied the only approved means of direct contact with the world outside. The fortunate owners of horses and carriages and a few students from the college whose purses permitted the extravagance could, and often did, disdain the customary modes of travel and drive themselves to Northampton, and even to Springfield, to shop and visit; the students more often to dare the adventure of calls on the not unwilling but somewhat secluded young ladies of Smith College. Except for these occasional diversions, the townsfolk were well satisfied to center their interests and live their lives within the confines of the village itself.

The restrictions of village life made for a common friendliness among the citizens which was everywhere in evidence. When you appeared at the grocery store to supply the needs of the family larder, O. G. Couch, the owner, greeted you with warmth, inquiring by name for each member of the family circle as he filled your order. With the same dignified finesse which he displayed when he passed you the contribution box in the local church on Sunday, George Kendrick, clad in his white butcher's frock, handed you your sirloin steak at eighteen cents a pound. As the price would indicate, this was not modern Chicago beef, but was processed by Kendrick himself in his own slaughter-house at the foot of the Amity Street hill. The morning train on the New London Northern Railroad which regularly carried a sociable group of citizens on shopping and other business expeditions to the outside world was known as " Hastings's train " because the bewhiskered conductor was a resident of the town. The local *Amherst Record* of those days constantly reminded us that it was " Hastings's train " that was late, or that ran off the track, an accident all too common on that particular road which, even for those days, was commonly regarded as backward.

In most ways Amherst differed little from countless other small towns which dotted the New England countryside. It had its leaders, its loafers, and its characters, as did others. Austin Dickinson, with his visions of beauty, planned and planted and made possible the lovelier Amherst, and in particular the college campus so deeply admired by later generations. Jim Davis, the English cobbler and town philosopher, debated the affairs of town, state, nation, and universe with every customer, whether the humblest citizen or college professor, as he tapped his visitor's wearing shoes. Squatty, thick-set Henry Jackson, a few shades darker than the inevitable cigar butt that protruded from his big red lips, daily drove his lumbering two, and sometimes four, horse team to the railroad station or Northampton, conveying to local stores and householders eagerly awaited goods deposited by passing freight trains on railroad platforms. " Pete " Fay, rosy-cheeked, smiling and blustering, and with an untamed tongue controlled with difficulty when lady passengers were aboard, guided with an air of unfeigned superiority the plodding horses of Paige's famous stagecoach to and from the local station and on the long trek to Northampton and return.

But in one important respect Amherst differed distinctly from most New England towns of its size. It was an academic town; and the presence of Amherst College on the south and the Massachusetts Agricultural College on the north affected all strata of town life, and by developing a wider and more intelligent interest in matters not purely local, lifted the cultural level above that generally found in New England villages of the time. To be sure the " Aggie," as the state college was commonly known, was then somewhat moribund and wholly unlike the first-class and influential institution it was later to become. Indeed only a few years earlier the trustees of that struggling college in desperation had sought to persuade the authorities of Amherst College that a merger would redound to the best interests of both. But there were on its faculty several men of outstanding ability and worth, who measured up favorably with the much larger group associated with the college on the hill. Both groups of professors took an active interest in town affairs, and their judgments were freely sought by the town fathers, who regarded them neither as intruding intellectuals nor as highbrows. A common friendliness between town and gown prevailed, broken only occasionally when the students went on larks which stirred the temporary ire of the town's officials.

Altogether Amherst in that period was a comfortable place in which to live. It was truly a democratic town. Class and race distinctions counted for little, practically for nothing to those of us of younger years. The intimacies of restricted village life prompted us to seek among our mates that indefinable something, "stuff" if you will, which youth instinctively recognizes, and when we found it the possessors remained our friends for life.

It was in this New England college town that I was privileged to pass the days of my youth. And it remained my home town for several years beyond the close of my college days. Here in 1874 my mother, with her brood of seven small children, arrived to begin life anew after the sudden death of my father. For fifteen years my father had been a merchant in India, where he had met with more than ordinary success. The family home at Malabar Hill, just outside of Bombay, had long been a gathering place for American travelers and English officials residing near by or passing through the busy seaport on their way to and from their stations. Lord Napier was a frequent visitor. David Livingstone had made it his headquarters before his venture into the wilds of Africa, and my father had helped generously in fitting him out for the trip. Richard Henry Dana, the author of *Two Years before the Mast*, discovered when he lay seriously ill on a ship in the harbor, had been carried there and nursed back to health and vigor. But the strain of India's relentless sun, coupled with years of hard work, had begun to exact its toll of father and mother alike. On several occasions my mother had been obliged to seek relief by sea voyages and trips to France. Finally it was decided that the India chapter must end and a new one be begun back in the homeland.

In due time the new home was established in Orange, New Jersey, where on June 6, 1871, I was born. My father had made all his plans for starting business in New York City. Offices had been engaged, and a new house was in process of construction in Orange. He was still young and full of vigor. Since his affairs in India had prospered well of late, he had seemingly ample means with which to undertake the new venture. But the strain of India had depleted his vitality more than he at first realized, and he had sought the professional help of one of New York's most noted physicians. While under this man's care, but with assurance that within a reasonable time his full health would be restored, he received the stunning news that through the duplicity of a native Hindu connected with the Bombay firm the business had been wrecked and all its assets swept away. Only a week or two more and my father's interest in the firm would have ceased and his money invested in it would have been withdrawn. In his weakened condition this heavy blow proved too much. His death followed shortly, and my mother, long accustomed to a life of ease and semi-luxury, faced the future penniless and with seven small children, the youngest only six months old, for whom provision must be made. In her distress she turned at once for guidance to my grandfather, William Augustus Stearns, then president of Amherst College. It was on his advice that she came to Amherst with the thought of opening a home-school for girls.

Of our first and temporary home on Amity Street, in the house more recently occupied by Dr. Haskell, my memories are few and hazy. I was only two years old when we first took up our residence there and but four when we left it. Under such conditions memory can supply little in the way of reliable fact. Out of that distant haze two or three incidents only reveal their shadowy outlines. There was a picnic engineered by my older brothers, on which through great condescension I was allowed to go. It was arranged to provide special entertainment for the "Colgate boys," who had been close neighbors and friends in Orange, and through some whim of nature it left an impress on my mind of seed pods from maple trees. And there were those days when I waited eagerly for my brother Arthur's return from a private school on a neighboring street in order that I might strive anew for the prize he dangled before me of a soda if, as rarely happened, I should succeed with the aid of a home-made bat in knocking a tennis ball beyond the limit he had designated and carefully marked. And there was the night when I was permitted to attend at my grandfather's house the wedding of his oldest daughter, my Aunt Fannie. Time has not wholly effaced the color and glamor of that occasion, the first wedding ceremony witnessed in my young life. Little did I think as I stood in that room under the sparkling lights of the great chandelier, timid and scared and yet enthralled, that only a few months later I should find myself again in that same room, this time hushed but a bit perplexed by the evidence of sorrow all about.

The death of my grandfather in 1876, coming so soon after that of my father, was a doubly hard blow for my mother, who was still uncertain as to the future. It was because of him and in the expectation of leaning on him for counsel and advice that she had undertaken the Amherst venture. He in turn had a deep affection for her and had always treated her as one of his own children. And now he was gone and she must face by herself the forbidding days ahead. My oldest brother, William, was the only one of that group of fatherless children mature enough to sense the true significance of the situation. Shy and sensitive by nature, he was disposed to brood over

conditions he was powerless to remedy when he realized
they were bearing heavily upon the mother he loved. The
rest of us, ignorant and carefree, accepted life as we found
it, enjoyed it to the full, and gave little thought as to
whence and how came the food and clothes and shelter,
which we accepted as a matter of course. We sensed only
dimly something of the heroic courage which sustained
our mother in those dark hours, a courage that was never
to leave her and that in later trials we would be more fully
prepared to comprehend and justly appraise. At the moment the full significance of it all was wholly lost upon us.

In this crisis help appeared from an unexpected quarter.
Julius Seelye, already a member of the Amherst College
faculty, was elected president to succeed my grandfather.
Seelye was a man of independent means. He owned his
own home on College Street and preferred to remain there
during the term of his presidency. This decision meant
that there would be no regular occupant for the President's
House. In appreciation of my grandfather's long service to
the college, as well as of my father's welcome gift of a
College Church, which he had donated in the days of his
prosperity, the Trustees approached my mother and most
generously offered her, free of rent, the President's House
for her use for as long a period as the college should not
require it for official purposes. This magnanimous offer
touched my mother deeply. Here was her opportunity to
start her school under the most favorable conditions. But
her New England conscience rebelled against anything
savoring of direct charity. She had already taken her last
penny to pay off debts against my father's estate, and far
beyond the requirements of the law; and she could not
bring herself to accept gratis this exceptionally friendly

offer of the college. A compromise was finally effected. She would accept the house; but she would also pay a reasonable rental. On this basis the deal was consummated.

I was only four years old when we moved to the new and pretentious home, and my memories of the first years there are naturally confused. A few, however, are indelible, though it would be impossible after the passage of these many years to arrange them chronologically. We children were installed on the top floor, or " attic " as we called it, while the better rooms below were naturally reserved for the young ladies, if and when they appeared, who were to become my mother's pupils. This attic, associated with so many of my boyhood memories, was a large and rambling affair. On the front, facing the east and the Pelham Hills, were three rooms, a large one in the center flanked by two small ones with ceilings that sloped to the floors. My sisters occupied the central room and my brothers and I the two smaller ones. On the westerly side were two rooms assigned to the servants. Between these two sets of rooms spread the attic proper, a wide and spacious room, flanked on each side by store-rooms extending down under the eaves and the repository of trunks and boxes and excess furniture. These were full of lure and mystery to us inquisitive youngsters, whose imaginations were stirred by the faint oriental aroma that permeated the dark recesses and oozed with enticing pungency from cedar chests. The main attic itself, with a central stairway descending to the floor below and a ladder leading through a small opening to the unfinished flooring directly under the roof, supplied us with a perfect playroom. We had only to guard against the threat of the open stairway, protected by rails on the sides, and the large coal stove that stood in the center and supplied whatever heat was to be had in attic and rooms alike.

My own room, shared for a time with my next older brother Arthur until the departure of the two older boys to school or college or to Colorado in search of health enabled us to spread out a bit, was the room on the southeast corner with a tiny peaked window which brought me the first rays of the rising sun and allowed me from on high to gaze down upon the ordinarily humdrum world that lay beneath. But that small window frames a few pictures in my memory that the passing of time has little dimmed. Through it I watched with boyish fascination the passing of the New London Northern trains a short quarter of a mile away, their wood-burning engines spouting dense smoke and, at night, glittering with sparks as they climbed laboriously the steep incline to the Amherst station, or leaving a trailing and misty cloud behind as they coasted down grade to Dwight's Station and the piles of wood awaiting them there for the replenishment of their tenders. From that small opening I watched the great comet of 1882 as it spread its fiery and terrifying tail along the crest of the Pelham Hills. Morning after morning, shivering and trembling, I crept in the early morning hours from my bed and tried to figure whether or not that threatening monster had drawn nearer to my own earth to engulf it and burn it and me to a crisp. Here too in the early morning hours I watched the destruction of Walker Hall only a few rods away as lurid flames leaped skyward and floors crashed, carrying with them the priceless Shepard collection of minerals to the inferno below. And out of this same small aperture I craned my neck, again in the dark hours of night, to determine if I could the progress in my direction of the great fire which destroyed the main business section of the town only a short distance down the same street on which our house stood. To my excited boyish fancy each crashing wall marked a nearer approach of the devouring monster. It would be College Hall next; then the Library; and then — well, that would be the moment to flee. To this day I recall the relief which dawn brought when, allowed to inspect for myself the scene of the disaster, I discovered that even the old Baptist church, the nearest building to the ill-fated business block, remained intact.

Other associations with that old attic still color my memories of it. There on Christmas Eve my younger sister Mabel and I, holding tight each other's hands and striving vainly to control our fears, awaited at the foot of the ladder which led aloft the arrival of Santa Claus, whom we were delegated to escort to the lighted tree below. In awed silence we listened for the tinkle of the reindeer bells that would announce his approach. We swallowed hard as we heard the hoof beats of his prancing steeds as they landed on the roof and were hitched to the huge chimney — a perfect hitching post it seemed to us. And then as that muffled figure thrust its form through the aperture above and shuffled down the ladder, puffing and blowing on his cold fingers, we were on the verge of panic and ready to flee below for safety. But somehow we managed to stay and, aided by his friendly reassurance, guide him safely to the festive room downstairs. That he came to us garbed in Arabian fez and flowing gowns troubled us not at all. In fact it only confirmed our belief that ours was the real Santa, while the conventional fellow with flowing beard

and protruding stomach who deigned to visit our friends
was a second-rater — Santa's son indeed, for so Santa him-
himself had assured us. Nor did the absence of an older
brother as we gathered at the tree arouse our suspicions.

The sad awakening came too soon. The unbelief of some
of our friends in their increasingly sophisticated years and
the customary suspicions that invade the minds of growing youth had in part prepared us for the shock ahead.
But even so it hurt. Curiosity finally did its deadly work.
In a rash moment we decided to take fate in our hands and
investigate the interior of a mysterious trunk in the attic
store-room, a trunk fragrant with the spicy odors of the
East to which access had been denied us. With consciences
struggling against curiosity, and curiosity winning, we
tremblingly lifted the lid. And there before our eyes lay
the Santa Claus clothes, fez, robes and all. So ended that
happy illusion of childhood.

In those earliest years my playmates were chiefly sons
of members of the college faculty and boys who resided
in the immediate vicinity. For the most part they were
about my own age, though I came to know fairly intimately a few of maturer years who were friends of my
brothers. The circle widened with the passing of the years
until it included a somewhat cosmopolitan group. The
first money I ever earned came from driving our own cows
and the cows of several residents of Northampton Road to
a pasture located about a mile from the college hill on that
much traveled highway. These daily trips, by bringing me
into close contact with boys of my age who dwelt along
that road, extended the range of my friendships. I played
marbles with young " Newpy," a Negro and the son of the

famous Dwight, who had already started his career as
boxing instructor, later as rubber or trainer, for the athletic
teams of the college. Armed with a bow-gun I hunted
woodchucks, squirrels, and frogs with Jack McCarty,
whose mother wielded broom and brush around the rooms
and halls of our home. Occasionally big "Slim" Hoar,
whose mother did the family washing, but whose home a
bit off the main highway permitted less frequent contacts,
would deign to join us in our games or hunts. And we were
duly flattered by these visits, for "Slim" was somewhat
older than the rest of us and had already gained local fame
as a left-handed pitcher. But black or white, Irish or Yank,
these new-found friends were a clean and wholesome lot.
They had the "stuff," and the keen wit of the Irish members of the group was welcomed and applauded. We
played and argued and sometimes fought, but we felt in
common the binding tie of friendship and were ready to
plunge into the fray, if and when any outsider dared insult or threaten any member of the "gang."

New friends were added to the list and with increased
rapidity as time went on. William B. Graves joined the
faculty of the Aggie in 1874 and established his family in
a house on Lincoln Avenue, now the residence of Ernest
Whitcomb. His two sons, William and Harry, proved congenial souls. We flew our kites out on the sloping lawn in
front of the house and engaged in such athletic activities
as our limited years permitted. Arthur Jameson, whose
father was the local postmaster and whose older brother
was to gain fame as a historian, was added to the band.
And it was Hubert Clark, son of the president of the Aggie, who saw in us promising recruits for his higher purposes and finally welded us into a secret society having for

its objective the collection and study of objects zoological and mineralogical. Not all were chosen for this high venture. Nor can I recall, if indeed I ever knew, just what standards were required for qualification. Chi Delta were the mystic Greek letters which, carved deep on the smoothed side of a ten-cent piece to which a long pin was soldered, proclaimed from the vantage ground of our neckties that we were members of a select band.

The lure of the mystic, enhanced by Greek characters and so dear to the hearts of youth, undoubtedly encouraged some of us to accept the proffered membership in this secret clan. But there were other inducements not recognized by the founder but potent with us. The Clark home in the northern part of the town and on the outskirts of the Aggie grounds was one of the show places of Amherst. It included a spacious barn in which we were assured a room had been reserved for our collections and meetings. That was a real asset, and Hubert knew it. What he did not realize quite so clearly was that there were other assets which appealed even more strongly to our boyish fancies. There was the tennis court, for example, one of the very few of which the town could boast, gazed at with unconcealed envy by every passing urchin. There were also the neighboring orchards of the Aggie, loaded in their seasons with ripening apples, pears, peaches, and grapes. And last but not least there were Hubert's sisters, the " Clark girls " as they were popularly known, and commonly considered the prettiest and most vivacious girls in the village. Their claim to this high rating was disputed by some who favored the Hills sisters, who resided in another of the town's show places on the eastern slope. All of these young ladies were much older than we. I doubt whether they even knew most of us by sight. Certainly they did not count us among their gentleman friends. But we recognized something commanding and, to our boyish hearts, something very attractive about them; so we worshiped from afar. And now luck had offered us the rare chance of getting a bit nearer to those who constituted one of these choice groups; of speaking to them perhaps, or possibly — and here our boyish imagination hit the high spots — of playing tennis with them. Anyway, we joined. At least those of us who were asked did so. I cannot recall all of our members, but I do remember that the Graves boys were included, for it was only a year or two later that they were solemnly expelled.

After a short stay at the Aggie Professor Graves accepted in 1881 a call from Phillips Academy, where he served almost to the day of his death many years later as head of the Science department. At Andover his boys were enrolled as pupils in the famous school to which their father had been called. Nor had they been long in their new home when the disturbing news reached us that both had joined a secret society in their school. It was a serious group that met in the Clark barn to decide on our proper course of action in view of the gravity of the situation which so unexpectedly confronted us. But a solemn " oath " had clearly been violated. That was enough to shorten discussions. And so with severe but somewhat shaken solemnity, we voted to cancel their names from our roll of members and cast them out "forever." The thought that all of us, within the space of the next few years and under almost the same circumstances as those which confronted our expelled brethren, would break our " oaths " never penetrated our boyish minds. Our friends had had their chance, had been tried and found wanting; and that was enough.

But in spite of this blow Chi Delta flourished for a time. We made our expeditions about the countryside, roamed the Pelham Hills, the Holyoke Range, and the Connecticut Valley in search of insects and butterflies, birds' nests and eggs, minerals and arrow heads, all of which were duly deposited in the big showcase in the meeting room of the Clark barn. But a storm was brewing just ahead that was to spell our doom. The first whisperings came to us in a request from our expelled members that the specimens which they had personally collected, being their personal property, should be forwarded to them at their home address. This request we promptly and flatly refused to grant. All specimens were of course the property of the society. So we argued then; but when some of us later had occasion to shift our residences, the problem assumed a different hue. Protest as we might, Clark supported by a few faithful followers stood firm and vowed that not a single specimen should leave our sacred quarters. Heatedly demanding rights which we had with equal heat denied to former members only a few months before, most of us announced our resignations and withdrew. But we did so with real regret, for we had had our fun, had raided too many times to remember the Aggie orchards, had even played tennis with the girls, had collected not a few worth while specimens, and had learned a lot, for Hubert Clark knew even then as much about birds and bugs as did some of his elders who instructed students of the two colleges in Zoology.

Some of that youthful band were destined to attain no little fame in later years. Clark was appointed to the Harvard faculty, where as a member of the staff of the Peabody Museum he served many years and traveled in the interests of his work to far corners of the world. " Billy " Graves, after a distinguished record in both scholarship and athletics at Andover and Yale, became an outstanding surgeon in Boston, specializing in gynecology and winning signal honors at home and abroad. Harry, his younger brother, a scholar and athlete too, headed and developed the Yale School of Forestry and later became chief of the United States Department of Forestry. I was to see a good deal of these Graves brothers in later years. The family home remained in Andover till the father's death many years later, and Professor Graves and his motherly wife always treated me as if I were one of their own family. A dearer couple never lived. Professor Graves, who still served the Andover school during the early years of my headmastership, was an inexhaustible source of wise and friendly counsel and the most helpful and dependable of colleagues. His keen sense of humor coupled with his clear understanding of the potentialities as well as the limitations of adolescent boys enabled him to exercise on his more impetuous colleagues of the faculty a wholesome restraining influence. In his death I lost a strong supporter and a rare and understanding friend.

Chi Delta did not by any means absorb all of my time and interests during that period. Some of us, less scientifically minded perhaps, were lured by the athletic activities of the college and were already dreaming of days to come when we too might win the acclaim of the crowd by our own feats on diamond and gridiron. Baseball held the center of the stage in those days. Football was only just begin-

ning to shake its swaddling clothes, and Track had hardly
been born. We skirted the edges of Blake Field, where the
games were held, and gazed with awe on the figures of
strangely clad visitors who came from colleges far, far
away. To us with our limited horizons they might well
have come from Mars. But the wearers of the purple and
white were at least human. We knew them all by name;
and we had formed our own opinions as to their abilities
and limitations. Each of us had his special hero, or heroes,
whom we sought to emulate and whom we were ready to
defend to the last breath, and sometimes with our fists.
Still more the Amherst nine almost always included a rep-
resentative or two from the town itself, and this fact gave
added encouragement to our dreams of that far-off but
glorious day when we too might don Amherst suits and
step to the plate amid the cheers of an admiring crowd. I
can clearly recall my own childish efforts to copy exactly
the gait and mannerisms of Stuart, an Amherst outfielder
of some renown. Like "Babe" Ruth of a modern age,
Stuart was a slugger and specialized in home runs. And
that was enough. Whenever the opportunity offered, I
would follow him on the street or on the way to the college
church, cramping my fingers as he appeared to do and
swinging my legs as he did his. Once I could master these,
to me, essentials, I was confident that I would have made
the right start for the goal I sought — a finished ball player.

These early contacts with the "truly great" of the baseball world prompted us speedily to organize teams of our
own. Our hands were still too small to encircle an approved baseball. But a ten-cent OK ball just fitted. We pur-
chased several of the latter, picked up a discarded bat or
two, and organized a "league." Each league team con-

sisted of three men only, a pitcher, a catcher, and a first baseman. For fields we appropriated any vacant pasture lots we could find; and on these through the summer months were waged during the early evening hours of several days each week the contests that were to start us on the road to the fame of our boyish dreams. And when a year or two later we pooled our resources, collected the best men that the different teams supplied, and challenged the local high school nine — and with a ball of standard size — we felt that at last we were on our way.

But our activities were not limited to baseball which, after all, was a seasonable affair. Our fancy had been stirred by glimpses we had caught from the street of those of questionable morals who patronized the local billiard rooms, at the hotel especially. This billiard " parlor " was located on the ground floor with wide windows which clearly revealed the revelry within. The click of those shining ivory balls and the shouts of laughter that came to our tingling ears were a bit alcoholic in their effects. But to enter those forbidden precincts, where we had been led to believe the Devil lurked unabashed, was beyond our daring. And our hesitancy to attempt this venture was further strengthened by the commonly accepted rumor that adjoining this luring room of heavy tables, clicking balls, and shining lights was a door leading still further into Hell where to the initiates rum and whiskey were to be had for the asking — and the paying.

Long and earnestly we wrestled with this moral problem. And our conclusion was that in the game itself there could be nothing intrinsically bad. It was the surroundings only that gave the Devil his chance. Well then, why not better the surroundings and enjoy the harmless fun ourselves? But where and how were we to secure needed equipment? The tables especially stumped us. But in the minds of some of this group lay dormant traces of real genius. Which youthful imagination bore the blossom on this particular occasion I cannot recall. But one did; and the proposal now put forth by its owner captivated us all. All we had to do, he suggested, was to find some old tables lying about our homes, drive posts in the four corners, stretch several strands of tough twine around these posts and along the sides, and we would have our billiard tables, cushions and all. With that start the rest was comparatively easy. For balls we visited a near-by planing shop and had these needed articles duly turned out of hard wood. Another visit to the Bartlett fish-pole factory in Pelham, a familiar place to most of us who regularly sought it each spring for fish-pole bargains when the drummers returned with their shopworn samples, supplied us with some butts of fish poles which made excellent cues. In due season several of us had duly installed, mostly in cellars or barns to avoid publicity and embarrassing questions from within and without, the new brand of billiard tables, and a tournament was soon under way.

But somehow we did not get quite the full fun out of this venture that we had counted on. The associations of the game, which we could not wholly forget, coupled with the fact that we had deemed it wise to secure the secrecy of cellar or barn, made unwelcome inroads on our New England consciences. Again a flash of genius pointed the way of escape. Who was guilty of this bright thought my memory refuses to record, but to this day I take off my hat to the one who evolved it. It was a master stroke.

Most, if not all, of us were fairly regular attendants at

the Sunday evening meetings of the Young People's Society of Christian Endeavor. We could hardly be called
active members and we were actuated by varying mo-
tives. Some welcomed the chance to see and meet girl
friends. Some were propelled by vigorous pressure from
their homes. All of us enjoyed the chance the meetings
offered of getting together, before and after, to discuss the
interests that we mutually shared. And then there was, of
course, a nebulous inner feeling fostered in our several
New England homes, that we ought to go. None of us
could be called exactly religious. But there was one fellow,
who had not been accepted into our inner circles but with
whom we were all on good terms and who not infrequently
joined us in our varied activities, who *was* religious —
"pious" we called it — and who was the outstanding
leader in the Christian Endeavor Society. Arthur Hamlin,
the son of a local lawyer, was older than the rest of us and
already revealed to our envious eyes clear evidences of
an approaching beard. A bit "slow on the trigger" mentally and physically, he was recognized throughout the
town as a sober, serious, and high-minded fellow of solid
character and exemplary habits. The suggestion that we
should secure his advice in handling our problem met with
universal approval.

Hamlin was duly approached and cautiously advised of
the nature of our predicament. To our surprise and delight
he not only approved the venture, but even intimated that
he would welcome the chance of installing a billiard table
of his own and participating in our tournaments. With
this conquest our consciences ceased to trouble us, our
whole outlook changed, and tables, cues, and balls were
dragged out of the cobwebs and shadows of their previous

homes and given due respectability. Questionings from
the unconverted were promptly answered with the simple
statement that Arthur Hamlin not only approved, but had
probably the best table in our outfit. And that was enough.
From that time on our new recruit's peculiarities were
wholly overlooked and he was accepted as a worthy acqui-
sition to our ranks.

The fact that I myself lived in a school for young ladies,
the Convent, as it came to be called by Amherst College
students, marked me among my mates for a kind of distinction on which it was difficult to set a proper value.
Some envied me my unusual position. Others were equally
sure that only a " sissy " could survive it. All agreed that
my lot was at least a bit different from theirs. And so it
unquestionably was. There were moments when I gloried
in it; others when I cursed my fate. An incident will illustrate these changing points of view and the rapidity with
which such changes could occur.

I had been granted the privilege of accompanying the
Convent girls on their annual spring picnic to Mount Toby,
a few miles to the north. Duly enthroned on the driver's
seat of Paige's well-known stagecoach, I surveyed the
world beneath me with something savoring of contempt.
I pictured myself riding by some of my pals and could
trace in advance the lines on their faces that would mark
their envy and homage. And as Paige's horses trotted by
the Amherst House in the town square, there indeed on
the sidewalk stood two of the gang. Delighted I waited for
them to cheer. And cheer they did, or better jeer, and as
the lumbering coach rattled by I could hear above the
noise of it all the taunting words they flung at me, " Hey,

Softy!" "Oh you Sissy!" which cut to the quick. Gladly, had it been possible, would I have climbed down from my lofty perch and raced for home and shelter.

In the main, life in the Convent troubled me little one way or another. Beginning it at four years of age, I had simply accepted it as natural and proper. The young ladies who comprised my mother's pupils were far too old to interest me, though there were several in those early years for whom I had a real liking and who ranked close to my older sisters in the respect they inspired. But I saw little of them except at meals, and at such times my mind was too much on the food before me or the prospects just beyond to permit their presence to interest or worry me. But in one way that life did offer something different from that of my friends outside. It gave me new and wider contacts, generally indirect, with college students especially, with whom otherwise I would have had little in common. And the new activities which these contacts fostered were promptly and gladly shared with my mates to our mutual satisfaction, though occasionally to my own misfortune. For if my mother's pupils were not interested in me as a male, they early discovered that I might serve their purposes as a messenger boy. That discovery spelled for me adventure, danger, and eventually humiliation and distress. But the adventure and danger made strong appeal, while the possibility of humiliation and distress never entered my head.

The location of the Convent on the very edge of the main college campus made it necessary for my mother to impose some pretty stiff rules governing the conduct of her charges with relation especially to their attitude and behavior towards the college students. But there were always one or two girls who had developed interests in individual members of the undergraduate body, interests which were reciprocated to the full. Hence the discovery that I could perhaps be used as a vehicle of communication proved a very real and welcome discovery. My memory as to just when or by whom or to whom the first message was sent is hazy. What I do recall is that I accepted under due pressure, and for a consideration, the hazardous task. And I am not likely to forget the final venture and its tragic end. Nor am I unaware of the fact that this unholy job brought me into immediate touch with more than one girl-sick undergraduate who was destined in later years to attain more than ordinary fame.

Anna Barkley, a strikingly handsome girl from Baltimore, had developed a keen interest in one of my brother Arthur's fraternity brothers, "Bob" Lansing by name. Lansing, destined to win later fame as Secretary of State in President Wilson's war cabinet, was generally regarded as the handsome man of the college. He had not then developed the scholarly tastes of maturer years, but he was a tennis player of some skill, and as he always played in a sleeveless athletic shirt which enabled him to display his well-rounded and bronzed arms — a garb considered a bit advanced for those early days — he was in a strategic position to win the attention, if not admiration, of passing members of the fairer sex who were privileged to see him in action. Whether or not Anna Barkley first saw him under these enticing conditions I never knew. What I did not know then, but discovered later, was that however started the interest had become a mutual one, a very real affair in fact, leading eventually to an engagement, which was rudely terminated only a day or two before the for-

mally announced wedding was to have taken place and by
the receipt on the part of the groom-to-be of a telegram
conveying the stunning news that the young lady in question had married another, and an earlier, lover. But all this
was in the unknown future when I shouldered my special
task. The running rate paid for my services was, as nearly
as I can recall, the huge sum of five cents, collected only
when I could supply trustworthy assurance that the message had been safely delivered. In this particular venture
I managed to come through unscathed. The number of
messages so delivered is not recorded.

Many years later, when I was serving as headmaster of
Phillips Academy in Andover, the Lansing-Barkley romance and my part in it were revived in memory in a most
amusing and unexpected way. A father of a prospective
pupil entered my office to discuss the requirements of admission for his son. He told me that his name was Barkley
and that he lived in Baltimore. The combination of name
and place aroused my suspicions, but I cautiously held my
peace as I made mental notes and tried to figure out just
how my story would be received if, as I was about ready to
believe, my visitor were a near relative of my one-time em-
ployer. He was a tall and handsome fellow with a frank
and straightforward way about him that convinced me
that he would prove a good sport and I decided to try him
out. We had settled the arrangements for the admission of
the boy and had turned to a discussion of the political
situation of the day. Woodrow Wilson was then occupying
the President's chair in Washington and was at the height
of his fame. The name of his Secretary of State, the Honorable Robert E. Lansing, appeared almost daily in the newspapers. Naturally these names were included in our con-

versation. Gathering my courage, I ventured: " I wonder
if by any chance you are related to a girl who once attended my mother's school in Amherst? Her name was
Anna Barkley and she came from Baltimore."

" I'm only her brother," was his quick response.

" Well then," I added, " do you realize how close your
sister once came to making your family famous? "

A broad smile spread over his face and he almost
shouted: " Do I? You bet I do. We all do; and we haven't
forgiven her yet. *She* threw him down. It was all her fault,
too. And if she hadn't we might all be sitting pretty down
in Washington today."

He laughed heartily as I related to him the story of those
earlier Amherst days. " Just wait till I see Anna. She'll
never hear the last of this," was his parting shot as he left
the room.

Another " affair " in which I accepted silent partnership
was that of William Whiting and Lyda — probably Lydia
— Scranton. And this one proved my undoing. " Billy "
Whiting achieved considerable fame in later years as mayor
of his native city, Holyoke Massachusetts, and as Secretary of Commerce in President Coolidge's cabinet. The
young lady whose attractions caught his fancy was the
daughter of the then United States Senator from Pennsylvania. Nature had endowed her with generous physical
proportions, which had earned her among the college student body the somewhat dubious title of the " Great Eastern," a name to be conjured with at that time as belonging
to the largest vessel afloat. My messenger service was
sought by both parties involved and was accepted at the
prevailing rates. For how long the service was rendered I
cannot recall. I only know that it ended in disaster to me

and something savoring of disaster to the lady involved. Having successfully transferred a note to Whiting, I requested payment from the sender. For some unaccountable reason Lyda declined to pay. Protests and heated argument followed, but with no satisfactory results. Finally my redheaded temper got the better of me, and stung by a sense of injustice, I fairly screamed in the face of the obdurate debtor, "You Great Eastern!" An hysterical outburst from the wounded victim gave evidence that the shot had gone home. A bit terrified, I fled. And she fled, too, but straight to my mother, where between sobs she told of the gross insult bestowed on her. But her anger had blinded her to the probable outcome of her tactless revelation.

With her customary common sense my good mother listened to the hectic tale and promptly decided that there was another and perhaps a more interesting side of the story, which it would be well for her to know. Lyda was wholly unprepared for an attack of this nature, and in response to some very direct and pointed questions broke down completely and unfolded the whole secret in detail. What her punishment was I can only guess. My own was swift and effective. Supperless and tingling from a sound and deserved spanking, I was sent to bed to await with apprehension my mother's regular evening visit to hear me say my prayers. With tact and telling firmness she pointed out to me the errors of my way, making startlingly clear to my thick boyish mind the fact, of which I had not even dreamed before, that in addition to my duplicity I was seriously jeopardizing the success, if not the continued existence, of the school from which we all derived our livelihood. That lesson went home, and my messenger service from that date ceased to operate.

The college students of those days had no special interest for us unless they happened to attain fame in the realm of athletics, baseball in particular. But there was one, known to us all, who though destined for later fame, universally roused our ire. In dress and manners Clyde Fitch was wholly unlike the average undergraduate of his day. His immaculate clothes, his gloves and cane, his spats and gaudy vests, and above all his " dinky " little mustache, seemed to us pure and inexcusable affectations. We branded him a " sissy," and our common ambition was to find some way, if this could be done with reasonable assurance of safety for ourselves, to muss up those clothes and bring discomfort or worse to the wearer. Every time we passed him on the street, or watched him as he ambled to and from recitations, that desire was intensified. In these later years it is hard to define the feeling shared by us all, but it was very real and seems to have had its origin in our youthful belief that here was somebody or something that could not properly measure up to the accepted standards demanded of a " he-man."

Fitch lived in the Chi Psi fraternity house on Northampton Road, just across the street from the northerly end of the grounds of the President's House, which then extended back of College Hall. Most of this space was occupied by an apple orchard, with a fringe of evergreens bordering the street. Here was good cover for the operations on which we finally, and after much deliberation, decided. In the slushy days of March we gathered a generous reserve of the muddiest snowballs our hands could fashion, and then waited for our intended victim to appear. When he did come and had reached the sidewalk only a few yards away, our dirty missiles flew. We were confident that Fitch himself would never dare to retaliate. But we were not so sure of the redder-blooded friends who generally accompanied him. For them we were always on the alert, and if and when they showed signs of entering into the fray, we promptly fled to safety. Eventually tiring of this attempt to express our feelings and to instruct our victim in the ways of real manhood, we hit upon a bolder scheme.

The President's House stood on a high bank commanding the road and sidewalk that separated it from the main college campus where most of the recitation buildings were located. From immediately in front of it a walk led to the college grounds, and joined a cross walk which ran from the corner of Northampton Road to this point. The house stood then at the apex of a triangle, and the student body in general used the straight and shorter path. A few with fair regularity could be counted on to take the longer route, which permitted them to pass within a few yards of the Convent walls and its windows where glimpses of blushing faces could sometimes be had. Naturally it was the " fussers " who chiefly patronized this more interesting, if longer, trail. Fitch was not exactly a " fusser," but some of his friends were, and he had been known to go this way. Anyway there was a chance at least that we could successfully carry out our bolder scheme.

When the melting snow was of just the right consistency we rolled the largest snowball that our combined strength permitted and carefully deposited it on the upper edge of the bank between the house and the adjoining Library building. Day after day at dusk, when the students were passing to and from their late afternoon recitations, we hid behind it and hopefully waited for the approach of the one we had picked for destruction. Days passed, until on one dark evening whisperings went the rounds: "He's comin'." We peered out into the gathering dusk and discerned three figures approaching. Whether one of them was He we could not be sure. But we had waited long and we were ready to take the chance. As the unsuspecting group came opposite us the prearranged signal was given. All together we heaved, and the huge ball of mushy snow went tumbling down the steep incline, breaking into countless pieces as it hit the sidewalk, while the intended victims leaped for safety. But our glee speedily turned to terror, as we glimpsed through the shadowy darkness three husky fellows tearing up the bank intent on wreaking vengeance upon us. We fled for our lives, down across the lawn, through shed and alleys, never stopping till we had reached the darkest recesses of the cellar. And there we stayed until the slowly passing minutes convinced us that our pursuers had gone and danger was over. Of one thing we were sure. We had made a bad mistake. Fitch certainly was not one of that trio. He never would or could have climbed that bank. But Fitch or no Fitch, our ardor in hounding him waned from that moment and we decided that we could best express our disapproval of him and his ways by ignoring him altogether.

Another character of signal but somewhat different renown who crossed my boyhood path was the famous Sabrina, destined to later immortality in college history. I had often seen that scantily clad bronze figure when in

seeming serenity she adorned the little flower garden at
the foot of the steps which led up to the old College Row.
I had heard the common rumors that she had been abused
and mistreated by undergraduates who lacked respect for
her proper charms, that she had been adorned by night,
first with a bonnet, then with corsets, and then with skirts.
I knew too that later she had mysteriously disappeared.
And right here my memory pictures become confused, and
I am unable to arrange with accuracy the chronological
order of the two occasions when the fair lady came again
under my gaze. But those two occasions at least are clear.
A shouting and milling band of students parading up the
street brought me in a rush from the house. The whole
student body seemed to be in that mob. On their shoulders
they bore aloft a wooden platform on which sat the goddess generously besmeared with whitewash or paint.
Where the crowd finally went to or what they did with
their prize at the moment I never knew.

Either just before or after this event, I had for some time
a closer and more intimate acquaintance with this famous
lady. The college authorities had wisely decided that to
leave her in her old and accustomed place on the campus
was to invite only further desecrations and more trouble.
And so she was quietly removed. In the big barn, a little to
one side and in the rear of the President's House, my brothers and I had installed a swing and a pair of hanging rings,
which furnished us no little fun and exercise and proved
a strong lure to all the youngsters of the neighborhood and
to some who lived still farther away. Regularly groups
would gather in the late afternoons when school for the
day was over and indulge in all the feats and stunts that
our fertile brains could devise. Nor did we confine our ac-

tivities to swing and rings. The adjoining hayloft and the
rafters well above it offered welcome opportunities for
tumbling and daring leaps. Regularly when breath and
strength had reached the near-exhaustion point, it was our
custom to adjourn to the apple room, as we called it, in the
rear of the main floor. Here were stored during the fall
months barrels of apples gathered from the adjoining orchard to await the approach of winter, when they were
transferred to the inner cellar under the house. The supply
was generous, and some of the varieties which proved most
tempting to us I have never encountered since. It was on
one of these daily excursions for customary refreshment
that we were startled to encounter, sitting proudly on her
pedestal in the far corner of the room, the bronze goddess
herself. We gazed on her with some awe, though hardly
with respect, until as we grew accustomed to her presence
we gradually came to accept and ignore her. Somewhat
later she was quietly removed, by the college authorities it
was rumored, and ere long had started on her hectic career
as a wandering adventuress and patron saint of such
classes as could steal and successfully hold her. Her remarkable story from this point on is too well known to be
dwelt on here.

Our activities in those early years were by no means all
in the field of play. My older brothers had started a collection of birds" nests and eggs, butterflies and beetles, shells
and minerals, which had been duly housed in rough cases
in two rooms at the rear of the second floor of the shed attached to the kitchen. On the single door which led into
these adjoining rooms was painted in imposing letters
STEARNS ZOOLOGICAL CABINET. My activities as a member

of Chi Delta had whetted my appetite for collecting, but
it was a long time before I could persuade my brothers
that I was old enough and competent to become an official member of this group of near-scientists. The day I was
finally allowed to have a case for my own collections in one
of these dusty rooms was a red-letter one for me. My chief
interest was in minerals, though I worked hard for a time
on butterflies, beetles, and other insects. But minerals fas-
cinated me. Armed with hammer and cold chisel I roamed
the countryside, the Pelham Hills and the Holyoke Range.
My standard of values was a bit faulty and was based on
color and brilliance rather than intrinsic worth. Of the
latter I knew little. But I did manage to gather a fair collection in which the glint of crystals and garnets and other
common forms supplied value enough for my gloating eyes.
And even my brothers, at first sceptical, finally admitted
that I had helped increase the reputation of the STEARNS
ZOOLOGICAL CABINET.

Just at the time my standing in the group was improving
an incident, fortunate for me, however tragic for others,
occurred which rendered my status secure. Walker Hall,
where was housed the noted Shepard collection of minerals which at that time was rated among the first three or
four collections in the country, was destroyed by fire. A
vault built into the stone walls of the building contained
many of the most valuable specimens, and these were
saved. But the rest crashed with the falling floors into the
burning pyre below, scarred and blackened and, in many
cases, broken into bits.

Admission to the ruins was promptly forbidden to the
curious while Professor Emerson and his assistants in the
Department of Geology and Mineralogy waited impa-

tiently for the tangled mass to cool and permit the work
of salvage to begin. When that day finally arrived, a crew
of workmen under Emerson's watchful eye began their unusual and immensely important task. Charred timbers and
other obstructions were first removed, and then the ashes
were carefully sifted, and every stone that appeared still
to have value was set aside. Day by day the findings were
transported to a place of safety. The discarded ashes, containing blackened chunks and charred remnants that appeared worthless, were wheeled to a dump heap to the
east of the ruins.

My interest in minerals naturally lured me to the spot
where these important activities were taking place. Daily
I watched through the burned-out windows of the ruins
the operations going on down below. I tried to guess what
colors or crystals lay hidden beneath the blackened surface
of each specimen uncovered in the ruins and carefully set
aside. But I noticed also that not a few of these chunks of
mystery were after careful scrutiny discarded and con-
signed to the wheelbarrows which carried the refuse to the
dump. At first curiosity, and later a burning desire to
possess for myself some of these discarded specimens,
prompted me to action. Morning after morning, while
these salvage operations continued, I crawled out of my
bed at the first ray of daylight and with box or basket made
my way to the black pile of refuse beyond the ruins of what
once had been Walker Hall. Here I searched and dug,
tingling with excitement as I uncovered an especially
heavy piece of blackened stone. Day after day, in so far
as my regular home duties permitted, I worked with hammer and chisel over these lumps of black, thrilled as every
little while my efforts uncovered some particular bit of

brilliancy beneath. The larger lumps I often broke in pieces since the smaller units could much more easily be trimmed. Furthermore, this procedure enabled me to discard at once anything that seemed drab or of little value. The refuse pile grew bigger daily, but the minerals themselves because of their weight generally drifted to the bottom where it was not difficult to extract them. It was a sorrowful day for me when the last wheelbarrowload of ashes was dumped on this Aladdin's jewel heap, though there still remained a lot of cleaning up to be done on specimens already deposited at home.

These new and unexpected acquisitions increased immensely the value of the cabinet collections. And they also increased its prestige among our friends. And they certainly gave me a much higher standing in the eyes of my brothers, who up to that time had been inclined to tolerate rather than to welcome me as a partner.

It was some years later that Professor John Tyler heard from me the story of my visits to the Walker Hall dump heap and the results. He was interested and asked if he might some day inspect the collection. I eagerly assented, and in due time he appeared and was escorted to the cabinet rooms. With increasing excitement he looked through my special cabinet, taking some of the pieces in his hands and carrying them to the window for better light.

"Look here," he said finally and with some emotion, "Emerson must see these. You've got some rare specimens here. Do you mind if I ask him to come over some day?"

Again I assented, and eagerly, for my pride was reaching the bursting point at these flattering comments from a college professor. In due time Professor Emerson arrived. With far greater care than Tyler had observed he took piece after piece in his hand and examined it carefully. All this time he had said little, emitting only " hems " and semi-grunts. Finally he turned to me and said in his deep but friendly voice, " You've done a mighty good job on these, but the college ought to have some of them. Would you be willing to trade some for others that we will give you? " And he added, in full appreciation of what would most appeal to the heart of a boy, " We will give you many more than we take and some with good colors too." The bargain was quickly closed; and my collection grew in a leap to one of generous proportions, though its intrinsic value was doubtless correspondingly reduced.

Apart from the college, the town of Amherst itself boasted of little in the way of intellectual and cultural activities. That was not to be wondered at, perhaps, since the college lectures and musical programs, which followed the common institutional pattern of the day, were regularly thrown open to such of the townsfolk as were interested. My mother had all her life been interested in music. As a girl she had studied both piano and singing in this country, and later in Paris; and she was determined that the education she provided for her girls should place more than ordinary emphasis on this particular branch. For piano instruction she engaged Mr. Hiram G. Tucker, the well-known organist of the Handel and Haydn Society of Boston, and his weekly visits to the school were periods of great excitement for the inmates of the Convent, both because of the new and fresh contacts with the outside world he brought them, and also because the noon dinner for which he regularly stayed was apt to be a bit more elaborate than usual, at least a bit different. Furthermore, he had a good sense of humor. My good mother, with the memory of recent sorrows still so sharp, and overburdened with the responsibilities of her school added to the care of her children, had little opportunity in those days to let her own keen sense of humor have much play. But it was always different when Mr. Tucker came, and at those noon meals wits were sharpened and laughter rang free. On such occasions her pupils saw a phase of my mother's nature to which they were not generally accustomed. They liked it too, and they liked her the better for it. Not that she could ever have been justly called severe. She was far from that, and the gentleness, friendliness, and tact with which she treated her pupils under varying and often trying circumstances remain to this day treasured memories among scores who still live to call her blessed. But the presence of Mr. Tucker, whom we all loved and came to regard almost as one of the family itself, seemed to take her out of her immediate surroundings and trials and to permit her to breathe again the clear air of earlier and happier and more cosmopolitan days — days when it was her pleasure to entertain with rare charm and grace at her own table the friends new and old who constantly frequented her hospitable home. Days, too, when she would sit before her piano to play her own accompaniments as she sang for her appreciative guests.

Mr. Tucker not uncommonly staged minor musical programs with his pupils carrying the major parts. But the great event of the year was his annual musicale, when members of the faculties and their wives and even a few from outside the academic ranks were guests and listeners while only his choicest pupils performed. It was a select circle indeed, and the program itself was of a high order.

But even august academic circles seemingly embrace a weak brother or sister occasionally, and it was in connection with one of these great events that my mother experienced a shock from which she did not speedily recover.

Among the most treasured of the family possessions of those days were seven letters written by David Livingstone from the heart of Africa, penned on the back of leaves torn from his check book which the writer explained was "the only paper to be had within the space of a thousand miles." These letters had an additional and significant value in that they had been entrusted to Henry Stanley, at the time he "found" Livingstone, to be carried to the coast on his return journey and mailed to my father in Bombay. My mother had had these carefully framed in glass and they were exhibited on rare occasions only. At the time of the musicale in question the Livingstone letters, in response to the urgent request of some of the representatives of the faculty group present, had been brought out of hiding and placed on exhibition on the mantelpiece in the parlor, where most of the guests were seated. That night, after the last of this select group had departed, the treasured letters were collected to be locked up again in the cedar trunk which regularly housed them. But to the dismay and consternation of the entire family only six could be found. One had clearly disappeared. For weeks we debated theories and possibilities, but that is as far as we ever got. The mystery was never solved. Perhaps it was just as well in the end, for when my mother died there were only three of us left to divide these cherished treasures, and that meant two for each. Had there been the additional one, it might not have been an easy task to decide which one of us possessed the strongest claim upon it.

Needless to say, the letters were never again exhibited to public gaze.

With Mr. Tucker available as an instructor, it was natural that my mother, in view of her own passion for music, should consider the possibility of uncovering some latent musical talents in her own children. My younger sister, Mabel, early showed ability and in time became one of Mr. Tucker's star pupils. Attempts by my long-suffering Aunt Minnie, to uncover any such talent in me ended in complete failure. My fingers were too stiff, or more probably my interest too sluggish. Whatever the cause, I got no further than finger exercises on the piano, and these to my immense relief were finally abandoned. The rest of my early schooling was a bit sketchy, though excellent of its kind. One of the first of my mother's pupils was Emma Moody, the daughter of the famous evangelist. For some now unknown reason her younger brother, William, passed part of the first year of his sister's enrollment under our roof. For a time an attempt was made to include us in some of the classes of the school. I cannot recall what those classes were or what subjects they embraced. But I do recall that we sat side by side on the rear seats of the schoolroom where lessons were supposedly prepared, and that our interest in upsetting the equilibrium of the much older representatives of the fairer sex was far greater than that in our studies. Consequently the experiment was abandoned. Thereafter Aunt Min, as she was known to all, and Sabra Snell, daughter of a former and distinguished professor in Amherst College, shared the none too easy task of trying to implant the foundations of knowledge in my none too receptive head. Aunt Min was wonderfully patient. Miss Snell, whose specialty was mathematics, was brilliant. Between them they managed at least to cram enough of the fundamentals into me to permit me in due course to gain admission to Phillips Academy. But that day was still some distance ahead.

Incidents of those earlier years which still stick in memory seem to indicate that, for all its simple life and ways, Amherst did supply events which, at the time at least, were truly exciting. I doubt whether any other town of its size could boast of so many and in some cases serious fires as occurred in Amherst from 1879 to 1888. During that short period fire consumed the Amherst House and adjoining Merchants Row, the hat factories, Phoenix Row, the Orient Hotel just east of the town, Walker Hall at the college, and the Palmer Block and Opera House where the present town hall stands. These conflagrations registered deeply on boyish minds.

One of the first songs I ever heard related to a sophomore at Amherst College who was arrested at a fire in what was known as the " Curragh," an Irish settlement in the northwest corner of the town, " for throwing a bean." As a matter of fact that is just what happened in actuality. Although the owner of the property appeared in court to defend the culprit, assuring the judge that the college boys had been of great help to him in removing furniture and valuables from the approaching flames, and that the beans which had been scattered in the process were mouldy and of no value anyway, the verdict stood and a fine was imposed. Blasts emitted by the *Student* in the course of the next few weeks failed to induce the court to alter its decision.

Perhaps this incident would not have remained in my memory if it had not been almost exactly duplicated dur-

ing my own college course when a classmate at a fire down
Freshman River way was arrested for picking up as a
souvenir a rag doll which he found in the rubbish. Instead
of turning this incident into song, the irate students made
life miserable for the local sheriff for the next few weeks,
gathering by night before his house, which they bom-
barded with stones, and the occupant with threats and imprecations.

The introduction of Pelham water into the town was
enthusiastically welcomed by the citizens, and the constant
breaks in the first-laid pipes furnished no end of excitement
to youngsters, who found in the flooded streets and nearby
cellars a new field of interest. Tar sidewalks, too, when
they made their first appearance, proved a boon to long-
suffering citizens who had for too long wallowed through
the mud and slush of spring days; and they proved also,
but for other reasons, a boon to the kids, who once they
had discovered that they could leave permanent imprints
on the new-laid walks before the hardening process had
advanced too far, lost no opportunity to do so. Rumors that
the new Massachusetts Central Railroad was being started
in the vicinity of Boston and would some day reach Amherst brought anticipatory thrills as local newspapers reported its progress in our direction. To be sure it was to be
seven or eight years before Amherst was to witness the
great event of the railroad's arrival, but our patience was
strengthened by the assurance of the officials that this road
was to become one of the great central routes to the west.
Tiring of the limited excitements afforded by the town, the
more adventurous souls sought the enticements of Lake
Pleasant, a few miles to the north, where the Spiritualists

held their annual camp meetings. These questing youths were often ejected from meetings for disturbing or breaking the " contacts " reputed to exist between the mediums and departed spirits; but it was fun and that was enough.

One of the incidents that eventually shook the town to its foundations centered around President Clark of the Aggie and his interest in gold mines. Little else was talked about at the time, and all of us heard the numerous stories that went the rounds. Clark had been one of the leading spirits in town affairs. He had practically founded the Aggie and nursed it during its fledgling years. No citizen of the town was more respected than he, and his record as an officer in the Civil War had made him much of a hero in the eyes of his admiring Amherst friends. When this handsome, vivacious, and magnetic leader suddenly developed an interest in gold mines, his words were listened to attentively and his suggestions all too readily followed. I still have a hazy memory of him standing in front of the old Amherst House and exhibiting to excited friends specimens of shining quartz.

Before disaster finally overtook him and his mines, nearly everyone in the town, including widows and orphans, who could dig up a penny or a dollar had invested their hard-earned savings in Clark's gold mines and expected to realize fortunes. That Clark himself was the victim of some clever crooks, his best friends all agreed. Undoubtedly he was innocent of any evil intent to mislead his fellow-citizens, but mislead them he did, and when the blow fell, he could count on scarcely a friend left in the town. He was compelled to dispose of his beautiful home, and the family scattered. Mrs. Clark once told my mother in a most pathetic way that there were only two homes in the town where members of the family could be sure that they would not be insulted, that of President Seelye and our own.

Woman suffrage was just appearing over the horizon. My mother became involved in a curious and amusing way in the suffrage campaign which was being noisily waged in Amherst. She herself had been vigorously opposed to it from the start and remained so until the day of her death. Unknown to her, however, she was brought into the center of the struggle, but was speedily released. In checking up on the incident, as it is recorded in old issues of the *Amherst Record*, I find these interesting entries, the first efforts of the belligerent women having been directed solely toward securing a representation on the school committee.

At this state of proceedings, eleven o'clock having arrived, the twenty-two lady voters were ushered from their place of waiting up the aisle in single file, Mrs. Merrick Marsh depositing the first ballot ever voted by a lady in Amherst town meeting. Just as the last lady had voted, the motion to turn the box was carried and the moderator announced, " *Gentlemen,* you have made choice of Mrs. Mary E. Stearns for school committee." It seems that the ladies supposed they were voting the candidate whom the gentlemen wished to elect and the rumor that they produced the ticket is not true. The ballots were printed and placed in their hands and, of course, it required no further printing to spring the project. We understand that Mrs. Stearns has been duly notified of her election but decidedly declined to accept on the grounds that her health will not permit of the task and her principles are averse to women suffrage, as she does not approve of women voting or holding office.

Two weeks later the *Record* carried this item:

It turns out that Mrs. Stearns, who was elected on the board of school committee at the annual town meeting is an alien, was not registered, is not in sympathy with women suffrage and had not been consulted on the matter of holding office which she strongly declined.

I had always known of my mother's aversion to woman suffrage, but I confess that I was a bit puzzled as to just what the *Record* had in mind in describing her as an "alien." From what I have been able to gather, I judge that this may have been due to the fact that she had only recently returned from India, and as one uninterested in voting had not, of course, registered. I have been given to understand also that in those early years a resident of another state was regarded as an alien, and since my mother's home state was New Hampshire, there may very likely have been no record of an official change of residence.

The intensity of my mother's aversion to woman suffrage was well illustrated during my senior year in college. It had fallen to my lot to be selected as one of the Hardy Prize debaters, the debate being a part of the regular graduation-day exercises. Woman suffrage was the topic chosen, and it fell to me and my colleagues to speak in behalf of the ladies. My mother's strong convictions in the matter provided me an excellent ground for preliminary practice and we indulged in many and sometimes heated arguments, so heated in fact that on one occasion at least she left the room in tears, fearing that I had become an actual convert. All of this preliminary practice, however, availed nothing when the debate itself took place, for our opponents led by Harlan Stone, now Chief Justice of the

United States, proved altogether too strong for our feeble efforts. I think my good mother actually gloated over the fact that our side lost the contest.

From what has already been said it will be noted that for the most part my intimate playmates came from outside the family circle. This was natural in view of the fact that my three brothers were much older than I and had their own special friends. Sometimes I was allowed as a great privilege to share in their activities, but generally as an accessory only, and not always a welcome one at that. The youngest of the trio, my brother Arthur, was six years older than I, and in our chief interests we had much in common. He not infrequently took me with him on fishing trips down the Freshman River and on hunting expeditions through the pastures and woodlands that stretched to the Holyoke Range, where a woodchuck, a couple of red squirrels, or even a fat grey squirrel might eventually rest in our bag to reward us for the day's effort. It was he who roused my first interest in hunting and fishing, and it was he who also stirred my first ambitions in athletic lines. In school and college days he played on the football and baseball teams that represented the institution in which he happened to be enrolled; and that marked him as a hero in my adoring eyes. And he was always generously ready to help me in my early and stumbling efforts to follow in his footsteps. The grit and pluck for which he was famous in his day carried him far and did much to overcome the handicap he suffered from being somewhat slight of build, but they did not prevent him from suffering an uncommon share of injuries. Bones snapped too easily, and as he was forced to catch some of the best college pitchers of his day, and with hands protected only by the flimsiest of finger-less gloves, I doubt whether there was a finger left that had not either been broken or at least disjointed. To my boyish way of thinking these were wonderful assets. But not so to my mother, to whom they brought torture and added expense to such a point that in later years my own athletic activities were definitely curtailed and for a time almost prohibited altogether.

With my two oldest brothers, William and Harold, I had little in common, though I deeply admired them both. Of my three sisters, Ethel, the oldest, was too mature to touch my childish world. Annie, only two years older than I, was my favorite and won my deepest affection. But she was shy and none too robust in health, and hence could not be expected to enter into the somewhat rough-and-tumble life that was then mine. Mabel, the youngest of us all and only a year and a half my junior, was a boy in spirit and with the passing years became a constant and welcome play-mate on the home grounds. She dared to do anything I suggested, and the wonder is that she attained maturity unscathed. I tumbled her out of wheelbarrows in which I sought to run her down the three steep banks that broke our garden in the rear of the house, pushed her off of the upper floor of the barn to the haymow many feet below, and almost blinded her for life when she accepted my chal-lenge one Fourth of July, after our fire crackers had given out, to drop a match into a tin can half filled with gun-powder. To this day the picture haunts me of her black-ened face, with eyelashes and front hair completely burned away, as it emerged from that cloud of white smoke, and my ears still ring with the shrieks of terror that burst from her scarred lips as in pure panic I rushed her to the house and first-aid treatment. The numbing torture I suffered during the next few days when the victim of my rash foolishness lay with her face covered with salve and bandages awaiting the dread moment when it should be decided by the attending physician whether or not her eyesight had been impaired or even possibly lost forever I hope never to experience again. By rare good fortune no permanent injury resulted. But the consequences to me were definitely wholesome and the sobering influence of that gruesome experience drove out of me for good much of my too evident childish asininity.

Happy and carefree as was most of my life in those earliest years, dark clouds were gathering that were speedily to spread their deepening shadows over the home. I barely sensed them at first, though I was aware that something sinister and depressing was in the air. All too soon I faced the tragedy of sickness and death invading the family circle and taking their toll of lives near and dear.

On the opening of her new, and till then unheralded, school my mother was forced by circumstances to accept almost any applicant who appeared. And among the first to do so was a girl from the neighboring city of Chicopee on whom tuberculosis had laid its sinister grip and who had not long to live. Her parents were dead and her guardian had approached my mother to inquire whether his ward could be admitted and receive the care and comforts that a hospital would naturally afford plus the atmosphere of a home which the sufferer had long been denied. In sad need of pupils and deeply interested in this opportunity for service to a sick and bereft orphan, my mother accepted her and in due season she was given one of the ground-floor rooms. Here, confined to her bed, she received such special care and instruction as her condition required.

It is hard today to realize that at that time tuberculosis, or consumption as it was commonly called, was regarded by the medical profession as a non-communicable disease. Yet such was the case, and because of that fact my mother little dreamed of the danger to which she was so unwittingly exposing the entire household, her own children included. She was uneasy none the less, and at the end of three months deemed it wise to require the invalid's withdrawal. But the damage had already been done, and tragedy lay just ahead.

In the five brief years from 1880 to 1885 four of that family circle were to be stricken with tuberculosis, three to die within that period, and one, after making a temporary recovery, at a later date; and I myself, under suspicion of having contracted the dread disease, was to be sent for two succeeding winters to Florida. Only a sublime and unshaken faith in God enabled my mother to carry on during those five dreadful years. Yet carry on she did, and with such marvelous control and poise that even the girls who saw her daily had little suspicion of the inner anguish she was determined they should never sense.

With the arrival of this physically helpless pupil my oldest sister, Ethel, a born Samaritan, at once assumed the role of special nurse and friend. Day after day she would climb up on the bed beside her charge and chat or read aloud in her unselfish efforts to brighten a bit the limited hours of the patient sufferer. This in itself was bad enough, but the danger was immensely enhanced by the fact that the medical profession of those days, again with woeful ignorance, believed that the victims of consumption should be guarded against the supposed dangers of draughts or too much fresh air. In that stuffy room with windows generally closed, my sister was sealing her own doom. My mother was doubtless the first to note the tell-tale change, but the rest of us soon realized that something was wrong, and the increasing pallor and listlessness of the sister we loved was not to our liking. She was only seven-teen years of age when death claimed her in the fall of 1882, but because of her unusual maturity in many ways and her deeply religious nature she had come to occupy a commanding position in our family circle and had won, from the younger members at least, a respect and rever-ence above the affection we commonly felt for each other.

In the meantime my brother William, who had entered Amherst College with the class of 1882, was obliged to withdraw during his sophomore year because of steadily failing health. He had never been robust, and he had brooded too much on the sorrows and hardships which his mother was called upon to bear. At the last tuberculosis found in him a ready victim. In her desperation, for there seemed little chance that the miracle of a cure could be counted on, my mother sent him in company with my Aunt Minnie to Colorado, where he passed away only a week after his arrival. A year later Harold, the next oldest of my brothers, was also forced to leave college at the end of his freshman year and for the same reason. A sea voyage to the Far East did much to restore his health for the time being, but under the advice of the family physician he was in-duced to seek permanent health in a more suitable atmos-phere. Colorado was again the place chosen, and there he lived for several years in comparatively good health, com-pleting a medical course and establishing himself as a practicing physician in a mountain city. But an attempt to work back gradually towards his loved New England proved fatal. The disease, temporarily slumbering, returned with renewed vigor and claimed him its victim in 1890. In a way Harold's illness, when it first appeared, proved perhaps the hardest of the many crushing blows that fell upon my brave mother during those tragic years, for till then he had seemingly been the ruggedest member of that family group. If he should succumb, what chance could there be for any of the rest of us? Such was the thought, no doubt, that constantly crossed my mother's mind in those increasingly anxious days.

My sister Annie, only a little older than I and closest to me in many ways of all my sisters and brothers, was the next and the last victim of the scourge that ravaged our family circle. She had been a close companion of my sister Ethel during the latter's illness, but it was over a year after the former's death that Annie first showed the dreaded symptoms. Again the indispensable Aunt Min was called upon for special service, and in her company Annie was hurried to the Clifton Springs Sanatorium at Clifton Springs, New York. She had not been there long when I received the unexpected and to me not unwelcome word from my mother that it had been decided that Annie needed the companionship of someone of her age and that I had been chosen to supply this need. In due season I arrived at Clifton Springs, to the unbounded delight of my homesick sister. Without the slightest suspicion that there was anything in my own physical condition to cause alarm or that my mother was acting under the advice of our family physician, Doctor Cooper of Northampton, I accepted enthusiastically this opportunity for new adventure and the chance it offered to broaden my limited horizon. Here at least I would see something of the larger world that lay beyond the boundaries of my New England village.

A sanatorium maintained for the care of the sick, and in this case mostly elderly persons, was not likely to prove a place for adventure, and this I soon discovered. But at least my favorite sister was there, and that meant much. Fortunately I also discovered another boy in the group, Norman Williams of Utica, whose situation was very similar to my own and who was there to supply companionship to his invalid mother. Between us we managed to add a touch of normalcy to a generally somber place. Together we roamed the countryside, hunted and trapped squirrels, fished the neighboring streams, and at the risk of our youthful necks jumped on and off the cabooses of freight trains as they moved to and from the railroad station nearby. We lost our interest in this risky form of sport after I had rashly tried to jump the forward steps of a moving caboose, a daring venture since we regularly attempted for the sake of safety only the rear. My foot slipped and I fell with my head only a few inches from the grinding wheels, while my companion stood by paralyzed with fear. The sound of those grinding wheels haunted me for weeks. For the rest of our stay at the sanatorium we indulged in tamer sports.

Dr. Henry Foster, who headed the sanatorium staff in those days, was an elderly man of sterling character and rare charm. His white hair and beard gave him a patriarchal look. He was deeply and happily religious, as genuinely so as any man I ever knew, and his daily trips through the long halls as he visited his patients were colored by the music of familiar hymn tunes which he hummed or whistled as he moved from door to door. His wife was motherly and friendly, and this childless couple poured out upon all their patients, young and old, the pent-up affection of parents. They had a winter home in central Florida on Lake Charm, near the headwaters of the St. Johns river, and Williams and I never tired of hearing of orange groves and alligators and the deep dark hammocks inhabited by all kinds of wild life from gaudy snakes to deer and panthers. Increasingly, as these tales were unfolded, Florida became in our thoughts a land of romance and adventure, and when one never-to-be-forgotten day Doctor Foster said to me quite casually, "Alfred, how would you like to accompany your sister to Florida for the winter?" my breath left me and I could barely frame a reply.

The two winters that I passed in Florida still furnish the happiest memories of my boyhood days. For the first my sister and aunt were my companions, but for the second I was alone, living in the shack provided for the workers on Doctor Foster's orange grove and entrusted with the appealing job of keeping the larder supplied with fish and game. It was a rare experience for a boy of twelve and thirteen years of age and was full of excitement and novelty. But since it bore only indirectly on my Amherst life, it need not be dwelt on here. The news of my sister Annie's death, which reached me late in that second winter, had brought its wave of homesickness and lessened greatly the regret I would otherwise have felt at closing the Florida chapter and turning my face towards home. This time at least I carried with me a full store of tales of adventure to relate to my friends; and this proved a happy and time-consuming thought to play with on the long and ordinarily tedious journey north. The old friends were waiting and eager to hear of my latest exploits, and the old and familiar activities were speedily resumed, so far at least as one noticeable change in conditions permitted.

Most of my early companions had been attendants of local elementary schools. Now I discovered that they had been pushing ahead, some to the high school, some to private schools away from home, while others, abandoning school for good, had taken regular jobs in town or in the immediate vicinity. These changes, natural enough with advancing years, had their effect on the group as a whole and on me in particular. Life was clearly getting more serious. Not only was there less time for play, but on the part of the older members less inclination as well. Increasingly I was being driven in on myself, and increasingly I was being left behind by my mates. If I were to overtake and keep abreast of them in the future, it was clear enough that I must push on with my studies and, if possible, in a regular school.

Before I had left home for my first Florida adventure, arrangements had been completed for my admission to the last grade of the local grammar school, but that plan was, of course, abandoned for the moment. I had figured that it would be reconsidered and adopted on my return from the Florida sojourn, or that even the first year in high school might not be beyond my reach with the aid of some intensive study at home. But the results of the Florida investment proved disappointing. To this day I have never been able to figure the true condition of my health at that time. My guess is that my troubles were more mental than physical, and that the ordeal of seeing one after another

of my brothers and sisters wilt and die in such rapid suc-
cession had preyed more deeply on my boyish mind and
numbed my will to a greater extent than I then guessed. In
any case the following year was a year of lethargy and inaction on my part and one of increasing apprehension for
my mother, who decided that the strain of school work
and school attendance would prove too great to justify the
risk involved. And so I stayed at home, lacking the earlier-
day interest in wholesome and virile activities and finding
it increasingly difficult to participate in them. My chief
desire was to be near my mother and many an hour was
passed in her room where, stretched out on a sofa, I
watched her at her work, little realizing that my listlessness was adding to the pain of the fears and apprehensions
that increasingly gnawed at her heart already badly
wounded by the blows to which it had so recently been
subjected.

There was little in that critical year to register deep impressions on my memory. Study under the guidance of my
aunt and Miss Snell was continued in a somewhat irregular way. Some reading, mostly in history, of which I was
always fond, was accomplished, but in a desultory manner.
My chief diversion lay in a more practical field — the ham-
mering of brass, a popular activity of the day. The trays
and candlesticks produced could hardly be called works of
art, but they found a ready market among my mother's pupils and at prices which a little more than covered the in-
vestments required. How long this period of inaction
would have continued or what its outcome would have
been had not another figure appeared on the scene at this
time, I can only surmise.

Following the death of my grandfather, my mother

turned increasingly for counsel and advice to her brother-in-law, Cecil F. P. Bancroft, at that time principal of Phillips Academy at Andover. Fortunately for me, Dr. Bancroft had never known a day of illness in his long and active life; and he was apt to be somewhat impatient with invalids and semi-invalids in general. He had reached the conclusion that in my case coddling must cease and heroic measures be adopted. In order to look me over for himself and to confirm his judgment, he invited my mother and me to visit him for a week that summer at his seashore home at West Falmouth, Massachusetts. The invitation was accepted, and that week proved a fateful one for me. Yielding reluctantly to Dr. Bancroft's insistent demand, my mother agreed that I should enter Phillips Academy that fall, but with the understanding that if my health proved unequal to the strain the experiment should be abandoned. The expense involved was more than could properly be faced at the time, but this obstacle was satisfactorily overcome by an exchange arrangement whereby I was to go to Andover and live with my uncle and aunt while their daughter, my cousin Fanny Bancroft, was to come to Amherst as a pupil in my mother's school. Hence it came to pass that at the opening of the school in the fall I found myself in Andover, registered as a member of the junior or first-year class, and a member of Dr. Bancroft's household.

II · *Characters and Incidents*

AMHERST LIKE MOST
towns, I suppose, had its quota of citizens a bit different
from the ordinary run, whose marked individuality caused
them to be classified as "characters." The term itself is
perhaps misleading, for it was applied with little distinction to those who could justly be called peculiar as well as
to those with whom we happened to be intimately thrown,
and who in many cases went out of their way to reveal
their genuine interest in us and in the activities which
claimed so much of our time and thought. These latter became in a few instances not only good friends but integral
parts in our lives. Looking back over the years, it is hard
to figure just what the Amherst I knew would have been
like without them.

Of these outstanding individuals George Henry Davis,
George or G. Henry as he was commonly called, was in my
college days at least in a class by himself. George was the
proud janitor of the Psi U house, though the range of his
activities was not limited to the building that housed that
fraternity. Short and of stocky build, dark as the darkest of
his race, overflowing with music and laughter, George
found life good and lived it to the full. No one better than
he expressed *le joie de vie*. Nor was he satisfied to enjoy life
for himself alone. Others must enjoy it too, and he made it
his constant aim to see that they did. In his famous "broom
closet" in the rear of the house, and with the aid of stimulating liquids placed in his care by a few of the more sporty
members of the group, George made it his business to

straighten out the snarls that now and then developed between even the best of friends, and helped them to see the folly of their fancied grievances. In the face of his philosophical admonitions interspersed with peals of contagious laughter, disagreements vanished into thin air and wounds no longer bled.

From this same broom closet George extracted the materials for his famous " snifters," which he offered now and then at bedtime to a select few. The door would be pushed quietly open, and against the dark background of the unlighted hall would appear the grinning face of this dispenser of cheer.

" Don't you think you fellows better hab a snifter before you go to bed tonight? You've had a hard day an' a snifter'll do you a lot o' good."

The grin would broaden as G. Henry waited for the answer, which was seldom delayed. A few minutes later we would hear him climbing the stairs again, while the tinkling of glasses on the tray he carried assured us that the snifters were on the way. Those snifters were really pretty harmless concoctions, mostly lemonade with a touch of rum or whiskey, but the ingredients were blended in a way of which George alone was master and they went to the right spot. Just which one of the brothers actually paid for the material used we never knew, as it was generally understood that once a bottle was deposited in the broom closet the question of how and when its contents could best be used rested with George alone.

But above everything else music was George's chief delight. He overflowed with melody and it took little to encourage the flow. Let anyone start a song in his room dur-

ing the daylight hours and in a moment George would
appear at the door with broom and dustpan. He might already have cleaned that same room at least once before
that day, but the fact did not bother him. Joining in whatever song was under way, he poked about as long as the
melody lasted. If you started the song in the evening hours,
there was the made-to-order chance to inquire if a snifter
were not needed. But when a group gathered on the porch
on the way back from the evening meal, as it regularly did
on spring and fall nights, G. Henry was at his best. No one
could outsing or tire him, and no song, if it had the right
swing, could supply enough verses to satisfy him. At the
top of his voice, while stamping feet marked the time, he
would improvise verse after verse, often including the
names of individuals present and not infrequently touch-
ing on some of their personal deeds or whims. One never
knew what to expect, and more than once the intimate
personal touch was not without its embarrassment to those
thus immortalized. The riotous laughter that followed
these unexpected sallies served only to spur G. Henry to
greater and more unrestrained effort.

Several of G. Henry's songs gained special popularity
and were frequently heard during the daylight and evening hours around the campus and on the neighboring
streets as groups of students on their way to or from recitations and meals poured them forth with varying success
in their attempts to hit "close harmonies" and "bar-room
swipes." Among the favorites "Climb Up Ye Little Children," "Roll, Jordan, Roll," "Gather Up The Little
Lambs," "Now Ain't Dem Hard Trials, Great Tribula-
tions" were in constant demand and gave G. Henry just

the opportunities he welcomed for improvisations and the vigorous action with which his music was always accompanied.

" Brother Cheney, you ought to 'a been there," shouted George.

" Yes, my Lord," echoed the group.

" A settin' in de kingdom," from George.

" To hear old Jordan roll," bellowed the crowd.

And the rafters of that old roof fairly rattled as all in unison roared out the chorus:

" Roll, Jordan, roll,

Roll, Jordan, roll.

I wants to go to Heaven when I die

To hear old Jordan roll."

With his flair for realism George reached the heights with " Climb Up, Ye Little Children." Once that tune got under way George really went into action:

" De nex' blessin' Sister Mary had

Was de blessin' ob two,

An' dat was how de good, kind Lord

Goin' to bring dem chiluns through."

Chorus

" Le' me show you how to gather up de little lambs,

Tote 'em in your bosom

An' gather up de little lambs,

Tote 'em in your bosom

" An' gather up de little lambs,

Tote 'em in your bosom,

An' let de old ship go."

And then George would show them " how." Shuffling in and out through the crowd while his feet kept time to the music, he would suddenly make a dash for someone in the group, clasp the squirming and protesting figure to his " bosom," and continue his prancing while the rest of us in a mixed melody of music and hilarious laughter shrieked the chorus:

" Gather up de little lambs,

Tote 'em in your bosom,

An' let de old ship go."

Sheer exhaustion would finally bring these evening vaudevilles to a close.

Because of his numerous social activities, for he was in constant demand at faculty parties and other social functions, G. Henry was on fairly intimate terms with many of the faculty ladies, who frequently stopped to chat with him when they met him on the street. Occasionally these contacts reacted in ways that George found it difficult to interpret. On one of these occasions he was seriously perplexed and his face showed it.

" What's the matter, George? " inquired one of his friends.

George pondered a moment before replying: " Well you see," he finally ventured, "I met Mrs. Neill on the street this morning, while I was pushing my baby carriage, an' she said to me, ' Whose baby is that, George? '

" ' It's mine, Mrs. Neill,' I answered.

" ' Why, George, I didn't know that you were married.'

" ' Oh yes, Mrs. Neill, I goes home nights.' "

" And what did she say to that, George? "

The troubled look on George's face deepened. " She didn't say anythin'. When I looked up she'd gone."

At times George took seriously the high social position he had attained and felt it his duty to live up to its requirements, though the methods he adopted not infrequently proved embarrassing to those on whom he bestowed his favors. I have personal reasons for remembering one of these instances.

My fiancée lived in Springfield, and the wedding was to take place in that city. My mother-in-law-to-be was definitely snobbish in her outlook on life and was forever talking about " the great unwashed," in which group she was inclined to class all who could not boast of wealth or social position. Her consternation can well be imagined when her maid, having responded to the door-bell, announced that a Negro had called and was waiting to see her in the family parlor. Fortunately she had heard enough about George from both her daughter, a former pupil at the Convent, and me to realize that her visitor was an unusual character at least, and she came down to meet him. George had donned his Sunday best for the occasion, and his face was wreathed in most bewitching smiles. But after the first interchange of pleasantries, conversation lagged. At last in desperation Mrs. Deane ventured, " What are the students in Amherst like today, George? Are they as nice as they used to be? " The certificate system of admission was then in its early stages, and George had evidently heard some of the many criticisms to which it had been commonly subjected. His reply was slow in coming, but expressed a greater truth than he probably realized at the time. " No, Mrs. Deane," he said, " they're not as good as they used to be. Fact is, they've never been so good since they admitted 'em on perscripshun."

Of the same hue as George Davis, but with a different job to absorb his time and strength, big Dwight Newport, " Newpy " to most of us, claimed a host of friends. Dwight was the rubber for the athletic teams, "trainer" he preferred to call it, who gave boxing lessons on the side, and on Sundays as deacon passed the contribution box at Zion's Chapel, the Negro church supported by the college and located at the northwest corner of the orchard back of the president's house. Here as a small boy I had regularly attended Sunday School in company with other offspring of the faculty who were of my approximate age. Rush Rhees, an undergraduate in the college, later to become president of Rochester University, was our teacher for most of the time, the only one indeed whom I can recall.

The members of the College Church regarded Zion's Chapel as their missionary effort par excellence. More than that, they considered it a choice opportunity to show their tolerance and broad-mindedness in matters racial and religious. So they sent their children there for Sunday School instruction, offering them as vicarious evidence of their own liberal views. I am sure that this close contact with our dusky-hued friends did us no harm. Nor do I recall that we considered it unusual. Some of these colored youngsters were our good friends anyway, and we made grimaces at each other across the aisles, threw spit balls when the spirit moved, and snickered in unison with them when anything happened that amused us. On the whole, and I suppose largely because of the college connection, the atmosphere at Zion's was sober and restrained, in marked contrast to that which prevailed in other Negro churches of which we heard, and which were looked down upon by the more sedate patrons of Zion's Chapel. I am not sure that Newpy ever conducted a class, but he was almost always around, and his size alone had a restraining influence on us youngsters.

My contacts with Dwight in my later and undergraduate years had no savor of Sunday School about them. Then
he was athletic "trainer" and rubber, chiefly the latter,
and as a member of the baseball squad I encountered him
frequently. The smell of the vile liniment he splashed on
our arms and legs still lingers. It was bad enough to be
soaked in it after the day's game or practice was over, but
when, as often happened, the dispenser of this concoction
rambled into your room at night and proceeded to operate,
you knew that you were in for it, and that your clothes, bedding, and even the room itself would retain that sickening
odor till well into the following day. Newpy swore by that
particular brand of liniment and insisted that the strong
odor was clear evidence of its efficacy. We always suspected that he stressed this point to forestall our com-
plaints that he used too much liniment and too little rubbing in the treatments he gave our sore muscles. Dwight
had none of George Davis's flair for music and clogging,
but his good nature overflowed and his sense of humor was
keen. He was popular with all, but subject to constant
banter because of the emphasis he placed on his exalted
position and the important contribution he insisted that he
made to the success of Amherst's teams.

On our regular jaunts along Merchants' Row to the Post
Office in the evenings we passed the stands or shops where
several of our good town friends conducted their busi-
nesses, and with them we frequently stopped to chat or
loaf. John Musante, known only as "John Peanutta," and
his buxom and jovial wife poked their heads out from the
door of their little shop under Kendrick's market to greet
effusively any member of a college team who chanced to

come along. No friendlier couple ever lived than these two Americanized Italians, and none more than they won the good will of the student body. With his huge basket loaded with bags of peanuts John Peanutta was for years as much of a fixture at the games on Pratt Field as the stands themselves, and his excitement and glee when Amherst's representatives scored runs or touchdowns were as keen as those of the noisiest fan on the bleachers.

A little farther up the street Jim Kelly conducted a tailor shop, which early became the gathering place for members of the baseball teams especially. Jim was an enthusiastic fan himself and attracted to his shop others of kindred mind. Hardly a night passed that some of us did not drift into this friendly shop to stretch ourselves all over Jim's rolls of cloth while we discussed with him and his friends the merits and demerits of games and players. He knew us all by name and never tired of the continuous and oft-repeated gossip for which these informal gatherings were famous. Jim's town friends who joined us were a clean and wholesome lot, ranging from the local priest to hewers of wood and drawers of water. Jim himself was one of the straightest shooters I have ever known, and I prized his friendship until his death only a year or two ago. Over the passing years he retained to a remarkable degree a clear memory of individuals and incidents, which enabled him to bring them back to life to the delight of his hearers, even if the tales were not infrequently more than twice told. To listen to his stories as he pictured the heroes of the past and, punctuating his words with explosive laughter, related incidents in which they had played conspicuous parts, was a veritable draught at the fountain of youth itself.

Shortly after my graduation, I dropped in one day to gossip with Kelly in his shop. Under pressure from Professors Garman and Frink I had somewhat reluctantly agreed to accept a teaching job for the coming year, and the news had reached members of the old Kelly crowd. Jim was bubbling over with mirth and excitement as I entered and began at once to relate an incident of the morning. "You remember Ed Donovan (I'm not quite sure of the name), don't you, Al? Well, I met him on the street today, and he looked mighty sober for him. 'What's the matter, Ed?' I said. 'Has anything gone wrong?'" Ed, it seems, had been climbing the ladder a bit since the earlier days, and had graduated from a "bar-keep" to an alderman in the neighboring city of Springfield. In connection with this latter position he had also acquired an interest in the Springfield baseball club, then a member of the Eastern League. "Say, Jim," responded the despondent magnate, "have you heard what's happened to Al?" "He scared me," ventured Jim. "I was sure you had met with an accident or perhaps been killed. 'No,' I replied shakily, 'what is it?' 'Well, Jim, it's this. You know how many offers Al had to join the big league clubs. Why, I even gave him a chance to join the Springfield outfit. But Jim,' and here his voice faded away almost to a whisper, 'he trun us all down and now he's gone and become a damned professor.' Gosh, but wasn't I relieved," chuckled Jim.

In the next shop to Kelly's Arthur Bardwell repaired watches and clocks. Bardwell occasionally joined the group that gathered next door, but his wit while keen was not quite so wholesome as that of most of the others and his tongue was decidedly less controlled. I knew him only casually until, with a couple of friends, I found that he could play an important and useful part in a scheme we had concocted for a forbidden celebration of the glorious Fourth. Summer days in Amherst were apt to be pretty quiet and uneventful at best. So at least thought several of us, including Frank Mills, a Williams man whose family had recently moved to Amherst when the father accepted a position on the faculty of the Aggie. Frank had at once won his place in the Amherst group and was ready for any fun or venture evolved from fertile youthful minds. In this instance our appetite was whetted by an announcement by the town's selectmen that no noise or celebration of any kind would be permitted on the coming Fourth of July till after six o'clock in the morning. The selectmen were waving a red flag in our faces and we prepared to charge. Our courage for this high adventure was reinforced by the knowledge that a goodly number of the town's citizens of maturer years were openly voicing their protests against this too excessive prohibition, which they rightly believed could not be enforced.

Our plans were promptly and carefully laid. Plenty of noise and at an early hour — that was the objective; and the nearer to the town's center the better. The bell in the tower of the Baptist Church offered a strong lure. Could we get control of it? The son of the Baptist minister, named Child, was cautiously approached and consented to join us, with the welcome assurance that he knew where his father kept the key and would produce it when we were ready. Mills, who belonged to the Alpha Delt chapter at Williamstown, had been courteously given a key to the local chapter house for his use during the summer months, and as I had one for the Psi U house next door, we selected the cellars of these two houses for our center of operations, counting on making sudden shifts from one to the other if the pursuit became too hot. So far so good, but we decided that we needed some further protection if the full program were to be carried through successfully. Bardwell was one of the town's special policemen, and we had learned that he was to be on duty the night before the Fourth. So I sounded him out. As I had anticipated he entered eagerly into the plot, explaining with a chuckle that he had already been assigned to the beat that covered the main street from Merchants' Row to Northampton Road and would guarantee that we would not be disturbed for a limited time at least.

We had laid in a supply of the biggest fire crackers the local fireworks stands could supply, but were agreed that these were not enough for the type of racket we had in mind. Some dynamite would do the trick, but could we get it and how? Holland's local hardware store was known to carry it, but Dick Holland, the son who regularly waited on you there, was the town constable and hence under orders from the selectmen. Our prospects at the moment seemed none too good. Fortunately Dick, though an official of the town, was also a good friend of mine. He was older than I, but we had known each other for many years and, as I have earlier pointed out, Amherst was a " friendly " town. From what I knew of him I was sure that at heart he would be disposed to sympathize with our patriotic efforts to bring Amherst up to date. The approach had to be a tactful one, and I took care to sound him out before daring to unfold our plan. In the end the results were all that could be desired, and after swearing an oath never to betray him I was handed a carefully wrapped bundle containing a half dozen sticks of dynamite, which was duly deposited in the cellar of the Alpha Delt house.

In the dark hours of the night of July second, with the aid of the key which Child had produced as promised, we stealthily entered the Baptist Church, climbed up into the belfry, and attached a rope to the bell. Crawling along the ridge-pole, we dropped the end of the rope over the western edge, allowing it to dangle below just within reach of the ground, where we felt confident it would not be seen before being put into use the next night. In the meantime at headquarters we had stored another long piece of rope, which would reach from the church to our cellar, and which could be attached at the last moment to the piece which dangled from the roof. Our final act of preparation was to cut in half the several sticks of dynamite and insert the fuses. This we did as casually as if we had handled dynamite all our lives. Then we waited.

Late in the evening of July third we gathered in the cellar of the Alpha Delt house, having carefully unlocked the cellar door of the Psi U house as well. The ropes were connected and the end carried to the Alpha Delt cellar. Peering out into the darkness, we could just make out the figure of Bardwell as he strolled up and down his beat. As the last stroke of the neighboring clocks announced the advent of the Fourth, we went into action. The explosion of one of our dynamite sticks out on the main street shook the ground, and at once the church bell began pealing like mad. This brought the town fathers to the scene on the run. From our place of concealment we could hear them arguing with Bardwell, who noisily and profanely assured them that he had never left his beat, and that he could not for a moment imagine how anyone could have entered the

Baptist Church, the bell of which continued to swing and jangle as the member of our group specially assigned to the task tugged and pulled at the end of the long rope. The crowd in front of the church continued to argue and it was clearly time to give them a further shock. The explosion of another dynamite stick up back of the old Alpha Delt Annex on Prospect Street sent them all scurrying in that direction, town fathers and excited citizens alike, for the group was steadily growing in size. No sooner had they reached the scene of this latest outrage than they were sent tumbling over each other to the Northampton Road corner by another crash as our third stick of dynamite blew up at that spot. A few scattered fire crackers added to the din and the confusion, while the bell in the church tower refused to be quieted.

By this time we were getting nervous. The crowd was increasing and we decided that we had had enough. The rope was severed and the end hanging from the church roof carried around to the north side to cover our trail and the loose end pulled in and hidden in the recesses of the Alpha's cellar. When the din on the streets had finally subsided, we crept out from our hiding places and slunk away to our several homes. As I look back on it this incident marked the last and dying flame of my youthful muckerism. I take no pride in my part in the escapade, but it and others of somewhat similar type did stand me in good stead when in later years as teacher and headmaster in boys' schools I was many times compelled to put a stop to youthful pranks and round up, if I could, the perpetrators. I knew at least that the broken rope hanging from the chapel belfry tower did not regularly point in the direction of the place from which it had been operated, and that those who touched off fire crackers at a given spot should be sought in other localities than the ones where these Chinese noise makers exploded.

A little farther up the street above the Kelly and Bardwell establishments stood the Post Office, where George Merritt, the genial friend of us all, handed out our mail. And a bit beyond Deuel's drug store with its up-to-date soda fountain drew a steady stream of thirsty souls, who gladly exchanged their dimes and nickels for plain and icecream sodas and a few other mixtures which Fred Deuel was skilled in concocting. From the college athletes alone, whose thirst was never fully quenched, Deuel must have gathered in a fortune of no small size. Adams's drug store at the corner of Phoenix Row across the square drew Deuel's overflow, and Morgan's just below could be counted on to furnish some beer now and then if the right formula were understood and used. That formula was best known to the janitors of the several fraternity houses who, according to G. Henry Davis, had only to draw a wavering line by way of signature in Morgan's record book. Since Amherst was a no-license town, however, it was generally considered safer to patronize Northampton's bars when beer was needed.

One of our best and most understanding friends in undergraduate days was the rector of Grace Church just across the Common. Sprague was early accepted as a he-man. He played an excellent game of tennis and had installed a court, which was always at our disposal. His interest in baseball and tennis led him to attend every college game he could and brought him into intimate and friendly contact with the members of the different teams, on whom he bestowed freely his best favors. In off seasons or if the tennis court were occupied, his home was freely opened to us. Here we chatted and gossiped and laughed, for Sprague had a keen sense of humor and loved to crack a joke at our expense. He had a good one on me at the close of our senior year, and he made the most of it to my discomfort for many weeks thereafter.

It had fallen to my lot to deliver the class oration at the graduating exercises. At Garman's suggestion I had chosen as my theme an exposition of one of the basic ideas underlying democracy, to wit, that strength is developed under the pressure of responsibility, and that this is actually one of nature's laws. I included in my illustrations the historic story of Xerxes bridging the Hellespont, and pictured in vivid language his anger and subsequent lashing of the innocent waters when a storm had destroyed his work. By way of contrast I reminded my audience that the modern and scientific engineer with his knowledge of nature's ways planned his bridge to conform to the laws of nature so that when storms arose the supports of the structure would only be strengthened. The one great weakness in my story was that I assigned the leading part to Alexander rather than to Xerxes, and it was the Reverend Mr. Sprague who first detected the mistake and gleefully apprised me of it.

The strain and stress of the commencement exercises over, I was sitting with a group of classmates on the porch of the Psi U house when Sprague strolled by. Spotting me in the group, he stopped and waving his arm in my direction shouted, " Oh, you orator! Alexander's bridge! Alexander's bridge! Since when did Alexander build that bridge? " Still innocent, I decided that Sprague had gone off his head, though I had an inward and creepy feeling that something was wrong. My companions, whose knowledge of ancient history was evidently as foggy as my own, were as puzzled as I over the strange behavior of our clergyman friend. My course in history at Amherst had included nothing dealing with ancient Greece or Rome, and my only contact with that period of history had been a recitation coming once a week in my early years at Andover. My authority for the reference in my oration was based on an illustration in one of Garman's special pamphlets which members of his class were allowed to use. At the first opportunity I hunted up this document for a check up. Yes, there it was in cold, plain print, Alexander's bridge. Still a bit uneasy I hunted up a Greek history at the library — and the horrid truth stared at me from its pages. Xerxes, of course, was the builder of that famous bridge. Sprague and his friends to whom he promptly conveyed the news, gave me little peace until the story had become a bit worn and that was none too soon for my personal comfort.

My admiration for Garman was such that I never divulged the source of the information which led me to incorporate in my class oration this stupid mistake. That it was a careless error or misprint in Garman's pamphlet I am sure, but I had accepted it as gospel, the deed was done, and the special commencement number of the *Amherst Student* of June, 1894, in which that famous oration appears in print still records — and I know this for I recently checked up at the college library — that Alexander built the bridge.

If the ranks of the faculty and their wives were temporarily split by the race issue at the time of the Ninety-Two senior prom, they were completely severed, and for many years, by the famous Todd-Dickinson episode. Echoes of that affair can still be heard around the Amherst campus in these later years.

In my boyhood days and in common with my friends I had heard stories of a mysterious woman who with her less gifted but equally peculiar sister lived in the house next to that occupied by Austin Dickinson, the treasurer of the college. I knew that these spinsters were sisters of the treasurer and, for this was common gossip, that his wife and daughter Mattie, commonly regarded as the town's outstanding snobs, were a bit ashamed to acknowledge the relationship and treated them as strangers or worse. Eventually we learned that their names were Emily and Lavinia, and that the former, who it was said could occasionally be glimpsed as clad in white she flitted between house and garden, was considered the more peculiar of the two. We youngsters dubbed them both " crazy " and let it go at that, though we did cast stealthy glances in the direction of that house behind the hedges when we passed that way, and even dared believe that we had now and then seen for ourselves the white and witch-like garments of the strange tenant as she tended her flowers. Beyond that we knew little and cared less. Unsuspected at the time, one of these " crazy " females was to bring fame to Amherst in later years. But more immediately the Dickinson ladies were to stir up a turmoil in the quiet college town such as it had never known before, and to throw the citizens, especially the faculty — and more especially their wives — into opposing and belligerent camps.

The foundations for this ridiculous but tremendously real drama were innocently but effectively laid by Mrs.

Todd during her early years in Amherst, when because of her modern ways, her natural charm, and her popularity with the younger generation, especially the undergraduates, she had stirred deep jealousies among the conservative and strait-laced dames who comprised a majority of the faculty wives. Her ideas were too advanced, if not radical, her parties much too gay, her dress too colorful, her manners too free and easy. She played cards and danced, even with undergraduates at proms, — so said these gossiping females over tea cups, at their meals, and whenever chance threw them together. Their ire grew as they rolled each new and choice morsel of gossip around in their cheeks and waited eagerly for one that would enable them to go into action. And that one came at last.

The landscaping and planting of the college campus had long been a special hobby of the college treasurer, Austin Dickinson, but he had found few in the college group who appreciated what he was attempting to do and none in the earlier years who were willing or qualified to help him make his dreams come true. With the arrival of Mrs. Todd the situation changed completely, and Dickinson took new courage. Here was someone whose artistic sense and whose love of natural beauty matched his own. Here was someone who could give him the advice and counsel he needed to assure him that his ideas were sound and that the final results would be the best that careful and intelligent planning could produce. Mrs. Todd in turn welcomed eagerly this opportunity to bring her artistic talents to bear on the beautifying of the campus, as she had already done in the case of her unusual home. Together these two congenial and artistic friends roamed the campus, planning places for trees, shrubs, and walks;

and — horror of horrors, they were seen at least once in Dickinson's buggy and on the same errand.

Here was the luscious morsel for which the hungry and repressed gossips had so long and patiently waited, and they seized it with avidity and ghoulish glee. It tickled their palates, and like a well-known chewing gum of a later day, the flavor lasted. Like a springtime grass fire, and like that fire with more smoke than flame, the news of this sinister incident spread until it reached conflagration size. Enshrouding at first only the ladies, the penetrating smoke in time engulfed a few of the sterner sex — and the battle was on. Those who still retained their poise — and there were not a few of these — fought the flames with vigor or shrugged their shoulders and turned their backs.

But a new and more devastating fire was even then in the offing, the sparks of which were to be fanned into uncontrolled flame, destined through later developments to extend to the woods and to smolder for years to come.

The actual facts which lay behind all this outward turmoil are not for me to attempt to verify. After all these years I can only record the definite impressions gathered from common gossip and constant discussions of the pros and cons which took place under my own family roof. My mother was intolerant of gossip and refused to permit it within the family circle. But this was something different. The Todds were among our closest friends and had later become our nearest neighbors as well. Because of her wide contacts with the outside world and her greater appreciation of what was customary in the broader and more tolerant society in which she herself had earlier moved, a type of society which the restricted citizens of Amherst were unable to sense, my mother felt from the start that Mrs.

Todd was the victim of jealous bigotry and had promptly come to her defense. Further, she had learned from Mrs. Todd herself the details of the grim story as it continued to unfold, details unknown to and unsought by the victim's most ardent enemies. The more she learned the more vigorously she championed the cause of the abused friend in whose integrity she had unbounded faith.

The details of incidents which account for the later and more devastating conflagration have been duly recorded elsewhere and will not be repeated here. A summary of them, however, as they are registered in memory may not be amiss.

It was generally understood at the time that through her contacts with Austin Dickinson Mrs. Todd had learned of his sister Emily's poetic talent and of Lavinia's unsuccessful attempts to give these poems the publicity which both she and her brother believed they deserved; and that Mrs. Todd had gladly consented to inspect the manuscripts, pass judgment, and if she found them worthy of publicity, lend her aid in securing a publisher. That she did find them worthy is now well known. In due time, and after long and laborious editing on Mrs. Todd's part, the first volume appeared in print and was so widely and enthusiastically acclaimed that further selections were required to meet the public demand. With the enthusiastic backing of Emily's brother and sister the additional and difficult task was undertaken by the new found friend. It was an unselfish and financially unrewarded task on Mrs. Todd's part and was so recognized by Austin Dickinson at least who, as a gesture of appreciation, deeded to the Todds a tiny piece of the large and then unoccupied meadow adjoining their limited grounds. This simple act, a small price in itself to reward Mrs. Todd for hours of trying labor, would have passed unnoticed but for other members of the Dickinson family, who till then had shown not the slightest interest in Emily and her work.

The unexpected fame which had so suddenly come to a member of the Dickinson family whom till then they had ignored, or more likely held in contempt, aroused Mrs. Dickinson and Mattie from their lethargy. They had "missed the bus." But the "bus" was still within reach. Gathering up their skirts, they chased it, climbed onto the rear and eventually pushed their way to the driver's seat (we had buses with horses, drivers, and rear entrances in those days), ousted the driver, and took the reins into their own hands. The process was a gradual one, but it lacked nothing in "punch."

The first step was to win over Lavinia, Emily's distraught sister, who till then had been co-operating wholeheartedly with Mrs. Todd. Since she was recognized as at least peculiar, this did not prove too difficult. What means were employed to bring her change of heart to pass can only be guessed. Town gossips played with the topic, suggesting such devious devices as hypnotism, threats, blackmail, and deceit, but these notions were the products of minds too much accustomed to thinking in terms of unsupported evidence and hence were not generally taken seriously. But whatever they were they proved immensely effective, and Lavinia, turning against her former friend and helper, allied herself with her belligerent relatives. The ground was now fully prepared for the great conflagration which burst with all its fury when, under concealed but vigorous prodding by the Dickinson vampires, Emily's poor and deluded sister proclaimed that her brother had been tricked, possibly blackmailed, by Mrs. Todd into deeding her a meager bit of meadow land. She was later and under clever coaching to support this ludicrous claim by testimony in court, for her unscrupulous mentors had determined to go the limit and place on public record and for all to read a decision that would brand their victim a proved impostor. Clad in deep mourning, veiled, and the picture of injured innocence, Lavinia with trembling voice was able to convince a susceptible jury that her concocted story was true and that she had been grievously wronged.

At this point the fire leapt to the woods.

The unexpected verdict of the court stirred the tongues of Amherst gossips into hysterical activity and sharpened the line of division between the opposing factions. No longer was there a no-man's-land where the uninterested could hide. From now on you belonged to either the Todd or the Dickinson group; and these two groups under this new impetus gathered into their ranks members of both sexes alike. Old friends were torn apart, families divided, and peace and quiet departed from the otherwise unperturbed New England college town. Occasional friendships still stuck; and Mrs. Tuckerman, "Lady" Tuckerman known to us all, and my mother remained friends for life. This exception to the general rule was all the more unusual in that my ordinarily publicity-shunning mother had actually attended the trial, sitting beside Mrs. Todd to contribute such support as she could, while Mrs. Tuckerman had definitely allied herself with the Dickinson clan.

If this strange feud had followed the customary pattern of its kind, it would have shortly died a natural death. But it refused to die, and for many years continued to rear its ugly head. Even hostesses had to plan their parties and dinners with meticulous care lest inadvertently they should invite representatives of enemy camps. And it was not at all uncommon for these hostesses, when invitations had been received, to be called on the telephone and asked whether this one or that one was to be present, the inquirer frankly admitting that if the answer were in the affirmative she would have to decline. Mrs. George Harris, the wife of Gates's successor as president of the college, whom I had known in her Andover days following my graduation from Amherst, told me more than once of the difficulties she had encountered in trying to solve this baffling problem. I had warned her before she left Andover of the situation she would face and she welcomed the challenge, insisting that so long as she remained mistress of the president's house she would entertain whom she pleased, regardless of the local flag they flew. Several years later she admitted to me that her efforts had met with failure. The feud was still very much alive.

Looking back on those days of unworthy and ludicrous turmoil and weighing all the incidents that were responsible for them, one can only conclude that this sedate and semi-Puritan New England town was the victim of the same type of mass hysteria which had earlier swept Salem and had given it the unenviable reputation of being the seat of the witch-craft mania so deeply deplored in a later and more enlightened age.

Through all the smoke of this unworthy and prolonged strife, one fact stood clear, something admitted grudgingly even by the Dickinson disciples: but for Mrs. Todd, Emily Dickinson and her poems would never have been known to the world.

III · *Freshman Year*

As my senior year at Andover drew to a close, I found myself in anything but a happy frame of mind at the thought that I would be entering Amherst College in the coming fall. There were several reasons for this. Amherst was my home town; the college, its faculty, and its varied activities were well known to me; and the customary lure of the unknown experienced by the average freshman on entering college would be wholly lacking if I continued my education there. I could not bring myself to believe that one could fully enjoy or fully enter into the activities of college life if he lived in the town in which his chosen college happened to be located. Day students at Andover, at least, unless they possessed unusual qualities, were apt to be lost in the crowd and seemed never to enter fully into school life. At best they were at a disadvantage. Frankly I dreaded the thought of being classed in such a group. Furthermore, my old pals had scattered and those who were still engaged in study were well ahead of me, some already in college.

But there was another factor in the situation which weighed most heavily of all. During the four years of my Andover career I had been thrown with some unusual fellows and had made a goodly number of staunch and valued friends. Practically all of these were headed for Yale, and none was to be found in the Amherst delegation. The strength of these friendships was well attested later when the closest friend of them all served as treasurer of the school during the entire period of my headmastership,

while several others served as trustees. I could not bear
the thought of severing these prized connections, and all
through my senior year I pleaded with my mother to be
allowed to go to Yale. My last, and like the others futile,
attempt was a telegram sent as the Yale examinations were
about to be held requesting permission to take these " for
the valuable practice " they would afford. I dared cherish
the hope that if I could make good on these the summer
months might furnish an opportunity to alter my resolute
mother's point of view.

I cannot blame my mother for the position she took. And
before I finished my college course I was glad enough to
thank her for it. After all, Amherst had a very real claim on
our family. My grandfather had been its president. My
father had donated the college church. And my three older
brothers had all been enrolled there as students. My good
mother felt strongly that to allow me to go elsewhere
would be nothing short of heresy and not easily explained
to our many Amherst friends.

Fortunately there was one Andover boy who had entered late in the course and who, like myself, was unable
to realize his hope of going to Yale. Herman Cheney came
from a family in which tuberculosis had been in evidence
and it was felt that the New Haven climate would not
prove helpful. He had decided to enter Williams. Cheney
and I had played together on the school nine and had
grown to be good friends. We were also members of the
same school secret society. Since I knew he had no special
interest in Williams, I suggested that he join forces with me
at Amherst. Parental consent was speedily granted and in
the fall of 1890 we found ourselves sharing a small two-
room suite on the top floor of Hunt's Block, a bit secluded

from the customary undergraduate paths. Our hearts and thoughts were chiefly with our friends down at New Haven, and Amherst activities had little interest for us. We grouched and bemoaned our fate; saved our cuts and pennies; and when the combined savings permitted, headed for week-ends with our friends at the Connecticut college. Each trip only added to our restlessness and freshman year for us both proved pretty much of a loss.

Our determination to have little to do with college, and especially freshman, activities was strengthened by a bit of political chicanery we encountered at our first class election. We had agreed at the start that, if and when the time came for considering invitations to join a fraternity, we would stick together, even if that meant joining none. Several offers had come to us, but after visiting several of the houses involved we had come to the conclusion that the Psi U group came nearest to offering the type of fellowship to which we had become attached at Andover. Eventually, but not until we had almost given up hope, the invitation came and the pledges were gladly accepted.

Alpha Delt had just opened its new home, a yellow limestone house so far ahead of anything that the other fraternities could show as to put it in a class by itself. And the Alpha brethren had counted on that fact to enable them to take their pick of the prospects that Ninety-Four might offer. But just the reverse happened. The pretentious house, the polished floors and shiny furniture, and the somewhat dressy garb which the inmates felt called upon to don in keeping with their surroundings, had a chilling effect on the timid freshmen who were entertained as prospects. And in their thoughts they were disposed to wonder just who was to pay for all this glory in the end.

Anyway they shook their heads and found the somewhat uncouth but definitely friendly surroundings of Psi U, Deke, and others much more to their liking. The Psi U delegation alone, when completed, contained no less than seven men, three of them sons of trustees of the college at that, who had refused pledges to the fraternity next door. Naturally this was none too pleasing to the Alpha brethren, and surreptitiously they evolved a scheme which they felt would help them make good the loss and restore their prestige.

In due course we assembled at our first class meeting to elect officers for the year. Nominations for president were called for. A Deke brother promptly nominated a Psi U for this high office. Not to be outdone a Psi U retaliated by nominating a Deke. Someone else presented the name of an Alpha. When the ballots were counted, it was revealed that the Alpha brother had won and by a large majority. Nominations for a vice president were then called for. As before Dekes and Psi U's put up their candidates, while the Alphas named one from another group. The latter won and by exactly the same number of votes as had been cast for the president. Then for the first time the Deke and Psi U brothers awoke to the fact that the minority vote in each case totaled the exact number of their combined representatives in the room. Glances were exchanged, but nothing was said and the elections proceeded. But when the ballots for secretary were counted and the announced results revealed an exact repetition of the two earlier occurrences, Dekes and Psi U's went into a huddle. It was clear enough that the whole program had been carefully arranged in advance, and we decided then and there that we would have nothing more to do with it. On the next ballot we declined to vote.

The last positions to be filled were those of class football and baseball captains and managers. It just happened that between them Dekes and Psi U's had gathered in practically all of the outstanding athletes in the class. Several nominations of individuals belonging to this select coterie were promptly presented and as promptly declined. The class was in an uproar by this time, and the presiding officer talked angrily about lack of class spirit and sportsmanship. We held our peace and stuck to our guns. When the meeting broke up, we were forced to record that no football or baseball captain had been elected. Altogether this affair proved most unfortunate, as indeed those who engineered it later frankly admitted. But it did cement the bonds of friendship and good will between the Dekes and Psi U's for the rest of our course. On the other hand it kept us suspicious of Alpha Delt, and did much to prevent us from coming to know intimately and appreciate many sterling fellows associated with the opposing group, whose real worth we failed to recognize till later class reunions and the passing of time obliterated the hurt.

If the pretentious new home of the Alphas tended at the start to scare off a number of those who were supposed to be definite prospects for that fraternity it did not prevent the brethren in that group from more than repairing the loss a bit later. Harlan Stone entered our class late in the freshman year. He was a town boy and a newcomer, for the family had only recently moved to Amherst from Chesterfield, New Hampshire, and had taken up their residence on a small farm on the banks of the Freshman River. Stone had been enrolled at the "Aggie," and rumor had it that he had been "fired." The rumor was neither confirmed or denied, Stone himself declining to have anything to say about it; but it persisted none the less. With that independence of judgment for which he was later to become famous Stone refused to be lured by the glowing arguments of several fraternities that sought to pledge him. Instead he took his time, looked over the individual groups, and eventually decided to cast in his lot with the Alphas. College gossip insisted that the Alphas had laid a special trap for this promising prospect but this gossip doubtless originated among members of fraternities on which Stone had turned his back and clearly had no basis in fact. It did not take the class long to recognize the sterling worth of this late addition. "Doc," as he speedily came to be known, was promptly given the respect and homage that youth instinctively renders its superiors. For the last three years of the course he was our unanimous choice for the class presidency.

The football team of the following fall was sadly in need of a guard, and "Doc" was vigorously urged to come out and try for the position. It was some time before this pressure brought results, but eventually the candidate took his place on the team, where he proved a tower of strength. The story commonly accepted by his mates at the time was that "Doc" had frankly told the captain who had approached him that he would have to take time to think the matter over; that because of his late entrance he had extra work to make up; and that in any case he had come to college to secure an education and he could not afford to run the risk of jeopardizing the attainment of that goal; he would need a few days in which to figure out whether or not he could afford the time. So reasoned the embryo Chief Justice. Regardless of the truth or falsity of the story, it at least emphasized characteristics of this serious-minded student which were to become increasingly apparent throughout his college course.

It was only a year or two ago that I learned for the first time and from Stone's own lips exactly what had happened at the Aggie to the lasting benefit of Amherst College. The Amherst Trustees were holding their winter meeting in Washington, a custom started soon after the Folger Shakespeare Library came under their care. These meetings have been held either at the library itself or in the chambers of the Chief Justice. Committee meetings have regularly been scheduled for the latter. As had frequently happened, after our official business had been finished, we were chatting and recalling incidents of college days when Stone said something about the difficulty he had encountered in gaining admission to the college. He told us that because of his inability to bring an honorable dismissal from the college at the other end of the town his application had at first been turned down. " If Seelye hadn't been a broadminded and human man," he added, " I probably would have had to go back to the farm and give up altogether the hope of getting an education." He explained that Seelye found himself faced with the difficult problem of playing fair with the Aggie officials in accepting a student to whom they refused to give a clean bill of health and that the difficulty was finally surmounted by granting the applicant admission " on probation." " And I never heard anything more about the probation," he added.

At this point I ventured to break in. " Look here, Doc,"

I said, "here's the chance for you to tell us just what did actually happen to you at the Aggie. You know that the story that went the rounds when you joined us was that you had gotten mad at one of your profs up there and had knocked him down. You're among friends now, the Aggie profs of your day are all in their graves, and it isn't likely that the truth could possibly mar your record as it stands today. Anyway we'd like mightily to know whether you really did knock a prof down."

Stone waited a minute and then, as a broad grin spread over his face, replied, "No, I didn't knock him down, but I shook him till his teeth rattled."

When the laughter had subsided he went on to say that when he had been summoned to the president's office, where he was told that he must leave, he had assumed that it was this affair with the professor that would be brought up against him, but that as a matter of fact it was not even mentioned. Instead he was accused of several misdemeanors of which he was wholly innocent. "But the knocking down of the prof was really not so bad as it sounds," added our host. "There was a roughhouse in the hallway following a morning chapel service. We were all in a rough-and-tumble scuffle when someone grabbed me by the shoulders. I turned and grabbed him and shook him, and continued shaking him till I suddenly discovered who he was."

The indifference which marked my freshman year was greatly strengthened by another factor, the practical repetition in the classroom of work which I had already completed in my senior year at school. In Latin and Greek especially, while the actual text may have been different, we continued to grind away at derivations, constructions, and all the rest with little attention to the historic or literary values involved. And "Eph" Wood in Latin and "Levi" Elwell in Greek proved far inferior as teachers to the men I had had in the same subjects at Andover.

An experience which I had with Elwell certainly did little to encourage my intellectual effort. I entered the college tennis tournament that fall and worked hard to win the championship, spurred on in my efforts by the thought that if success were to be mine I would be granted a three-day absence from college duties to take part in the intercollegiate competition at New Haven a bit later. New Haven, and not the tournament, supplied the glamor, and to New Haven I duly went. The opening round left me the loser, and for the remaining two days and a half I lived with my old friends on the Yale campus.

At the close of each fall term Elwell was accustomed to split his class into two divisions based on the fall term's work. These were commonly known as the "rank" and the "stink" divisions. To my surprise I found myself assigned to the latter, while the other eight Andover men in the class were placed in the more reputable one. I knew that I had not excelled as a scholar, but I knew also that the others were no better. And I knew further that at Andover as well as at Amherst I had outranked most of them. Under the Amherst marking system of that day the term reports revealed one's standing on a 1 to 5 basis. Actually 4 was the highest mark recorded in practice, the intervening fraction being a closely guarded secret of the recorder's office. 1 represented complete failure, 2 low passing, 3 satisfactory work, and 4 excellence. When my report for the fall term reached me I found marks of 3 for all sub-

jects except Greek. Here my mark was a 2. Protests to Elwell availed nothing, but in Professor Frink I had a then
unknown champion, and before the winter term was over
I was duly promoted to the rank division. Frink himself
told me the story later. He had protested to Elwell that the
assignment was unfair and had been met with the retort,
" No student can do my work satisfactorily and take part
in athletics at the same time." Other members of the faculty came to Frink's support, and my promotion followed,
though with no word of explanation or apology from Elwell and no change in the mark as it stood on the office
record. That one 2 cost me my Phi Beta Kappa key at the
end of my course, though the authorities generously
granted me one some years later. Though I secured nothing less than 3's during the rest of my four years and only
4's during the last two, I could never quite offset that ob-
noxious 2, and my final average was a fraction too low to
permit me to attain the coveted goal.

The reference I have made to Professor Frink prompts
me to say something here of this unusual man and his really
remarkable course in public speaking and debating. Would
that the college had such a man and such a course today!
Without him and his enthusiastic and stimulating teaching
I sometimes question whether I would have survived my
early indifference or been able to secure promotion to the
sophomore year. Anyway he supplied the one bright spot
in that otherwise drab and uninteresting period.

Henry Frink had only recently joined the Amherst faculty. He had come from Hamilton College, widely known
in those days for the emphasis it placed on public speaking, and Frink was an enthusiastic believer in the values

to be found in work of that kind. In himself he was an interesting character and differed from the ordinary run of
college professors. An immaculate dresser, he was likewise
a bit fastidious in his tastes. On first acquaintance we were
disposed to make some fun of his seeming peculiarities,
but we early discovered that he was honestly and deeply
interested in each one of us and that he was a friend who
could be counted on. That discovery promptly won our
confidence and increasingly a deepening affection and esteem. " Frinkie " was definitely all right. It was rumored
that he had been disappointed in love and that his keen
personal interest in us furnished the outlet for pent-up affection within, on which some unworthy and misguided
maiden had turned her back. Be that as it may, we welcomed this affection when it turned in our direction and
under test proved to be genuine.

As I look back over the years, I am inclined to think that
Frink's genius was best revealed in his early, and almost
uncanny, comprehension of the opportunity afforded by
the college fraternities for strengthening and furthering
the work of his department. Here was a tool ready at hand
which he could use, and use it he did to the full. His enthusiasm and the confidence he had inspired in the student
body must have stood him in good stead, for I can think
of no one else who could have done such an unusual job
with such thorough efficiency. Very early in my freshman
year I had this all brought home to me most vividly, and
perhaps my own personal experience will best illustrate
the extent and nature of this man's achievement.

Almost as soon as we had been duly initiated into the
mysteries of our chosen fraternity, we were plainly given
to understand that the winning of a place among the com-

petitors, and even more the winning of a prize, in one of the public speaking or debating contests, which were then outstanding events in college life, would be more highly regarded and would bring more honor to us and our fraternity than would success in athletic lines. We could hardly believe this at first, but we soon realized that our older brethren were in deadly earnest. In freshman year our work with Frink consisted in declaiming once a term and before the class some popular extract from speeches of the truly great. The well known *Hamilton Speaker,* of which we made good use, was filled with these. And so were other books of a similar type. From these Frink would select with care a speech which he thought best adapted to our individual talents. Then followed the preparation, and that was exacting. To each freshman was assigned a senior, sometimes a junior, of his fraternity group to whom he was required to recite his piece no less than four evenings a week in order to be properly coached. Next he must and did deliver his " oration " before the members of the fraternity on " goat night." Here he was unmercifully jeered and his oratory duly ridiculed and picked to pieces. It was tough but immensely effective. Next he was required to repeat the performance in the presence of Frink himself and three assistants chosen from the senior class on the basis of their high achievements in the course. To one of these he was then assigned for three rehearsals, Frink having indicated to the one selected for this high office the special weaknesses which should be corrected. Only then was the candidate deemed ready to appear before his class.

Of the prize contests with pecuniary rewards for the winners only one, the Kellogg Prize Speaking, was open to freshmen. But it had its lure, and Frink lost no opportunity to enlarge upon it. And so did the fraternity brethren of the upper classes. The rivalry between the various fraternity groups was keen and noisy, and the gloatings generous when prize awards were eventually announced. In the meantime the part of the course that dealt with debating only was rapidly giving the shyest members of the class a poise and self-assurance that had before seemed utterly beyond their reach. But it was not only by debating itself that values were imparted. In preparation for his appearance before the class each man was assigned special readings of which he had to make careful note, both as to the extent of the actual reading he had done and as to the time invested as well. A carefully prepared outline must be submitted to and approved by Frink himself before the candidate was allowed to fill his part in the program. Topics chosen were regularly those that dealt with important questions of the day or those of historic and literary import. Through the exacting readings demanded we acquired more knowledge on these important subjects than we regularly did in courses in which they were supposed to be the chief concern. Books for our guidance were carefully selected and placed at our disposal in the library, and anyone rash enough to attempt to ignore them or deal with them even superficially knew better than to repeat the attempt.

As the course went on into the upper years it broadened in its scope. Declamations gave way somewhat in sophomore year to prepared addresses, though the sophomore Kellogg Prize Speaking contest was the chief lure and the goal. In junior year the Lester Prize for original essays or speeches furnished the impetus. And in senior year the

Hyde Prize for original essays and the Hardy Prize for debating, both scheduled on the official commencement program, represented the truly high spots. The winner of either of these contests was acclaimed little less than a hero. If he was forced to spend a goodly portion of his hard-earned cash in "treating" his less fortunate mates, he had at least the satisfaction of knowing that they regarded him in a class by himself.

Today, as I listen to the rising clamor over the place of fraternities in the life of the college, and am constantly told of the extent to which they have slipped in recent years — something that I have indeed seen for myself — my thoughts turn back to those earlier and happier days. And I find myself wondering whether in placing the chief blame on the undergraduates we are really playing fair. Geniuses like Henry Frink are not often found, especially on college faculties. Yet is not the opportunity which he saw and so effectively used still there? Has the glamor of intellectual achievement ever been clearly revealed to the boys of our time by a teacher whom it has gripped and in whom it has stirred a missionary zeal? Has the natural and generally wholesome rivalry between fraternity groups been seized upon, as Frink so effectively seized upon it, to further the development of the mind? Has any serious attempt ever been made by those in authority to relegate social and athletic activities and interests to their proper and subordinate place in the educational scheme, to help these impressionable youngsters in fact to develop a proper and comprehensive perspective in which they can see for themselves what is nebulous and what is real and come to understand the unsuspected values, so badly to be needed in later life, which only the fullest development of the mind assures? Classroom teaching by itself alone will always be only a small factor in the education which a college offers. The broader and more lasting education will come from without and from many unexpected sources. The character of the individual teacher is one of the most potent of these. The tools with which he works will largely determine the extent of that latent power. Amherst has in its fraternities at least one of these tools. Has it the men of keen enough vision and of strong enough will to grasp and use it as some at least have done in days gone by?

One incident will serve to illustrate the depth of Frink's interest in the human side of his students. Each year there appeared to be one man above all others on whom he lavished his special attention and affection. This favored youth promptly became known to his colleagues as " Frinkie's Pet." In my junior year the senior thus favored was regarded by his mates as something of a " mess." Just what Frink found in him to merit the favor bestowed we never could figure out. In the course in Public Speaking he was good, but far from one of the best. Generally he just missed making a place on the speaking contests. And that is what he did when the preliminaries were held for the Hyde Prize contest. Frink had done his best to develop this fellow into a winner and he was clearly deeply disappointed at the outcome. Meeting the loser on the street next day Frink held out his hand and started to tell him how sorry he was not to be able to offer congratulations. He was rewarded for this generous effort by a stony stare as his pampered friend turned his back and walked away. " That nearly broke my heart," said Frink to me later. " I couldn't understand it." " But," he added, " an incident which occurred the next day filled out the picture and

taught me one of the great lessons of my life. Still a bit
stunned by this unexpected rebuff, I was passing through
the lobby of the Amherst House on my way to dinner
when a member of the graduating class rose from the chair
in which he had been sitting and stepped forward with
hand outstretched to greet me. 'Professor Frink,' he said
with evident feeling, 'I have stayed over a day just to see
you and tell you how much you have done for me during
my college course. I can't begin to express my gratitude.'
Frankly," Frink went on, "I had never liked this fellow
particularly and was never conscious that I had done anything to help him. I found myself a bit shaken and had
little appetite for my dinner. But I went back to my room
and outlined what I think will prove the best sermon I
ever have written. 'Cast your bread on the waters and it
will come back some day, though not from the quarter
from which you have a right to expect it.' That's the
theme."

" Tell me," I asked him one night as we sat on the porch
adjoining his rooms on Spring Street, " Just what did you
find in —— to lead you to pick him for your special favors?
Frankly none of us has been able to figure it out." Frink
was silent for a moment and then he said with some feeling, " Stearns, I'm not surprised at what you say. You see,
I have always made it a practice to look up carefully the
records and backgrounds of the members of each incoming class and to pick out the one man who seemed to me
to be most in need of help and for whom I felt that I could
really do something worth while. That's why I chose ——.
He had had little chance to make good in his past and I
thought I could help him to amount to something."

That was Henry Frink.

These intimate and delightful contacts with members of the Amherst faculty were not confined to those with Frink, though on his invitation I not infrequently dropped down to chat and relax with him on his vine-covered porch after the day's work was over. The liability which I had earlier felt the home-town college represented turned out to be a distinct and valued asset, especially in my senior year. John "Tip" Tyler was friendliness itself and Professor Genung, especially when he invited me to join him in a stroll over the Pelham Hills, made me feel that I belonged to his inner circle where barriers between faculty and student just did not exist. Professor Garman's home was always open to us, though its distance from the college, the almost unbearable temperature of the rooms, and its very limited furnishings were not conducive to friendly and social rendezvous. But these drawbacks proved no obstacles when as members of his class we gathered there in groups night after night to continue the discussions started in his unusual classroom. Old Doc Hitchcock was, of course, a friend to us all, and many others like Cowles, Morse, Richardson, Todd, and Crowell made us feel that their interest in us was not confined to the classroom alone. Several of these had been for many years regular visitors at my mother's home, so that in earlier years I had already come to regard them as something more than members of the Amherst faculty.

The early nineties were for Amherst, and probably for most other colleges as well, a period of transition. Old customs were giving place to new. Familiar characters were disappearing from the scene. Traditions of long standing were fading into a shadowy oblivion. The last of the religious "revivals," of which Amherst had for long had her full share, practically ended in my freshman year when the noted college evangelist, the Reverend Mr. Sayford, conducted the last, and not too successful of his "pep" meetings. The Day of Prayer for Colleges, commonly known as the Day of Poker, was fast losing its grip. Mountain Day, a day set aside in the fall in order that students might relax and commune with nature, was increasingly found to possess other lures than those of the hills and was soon abandoned. The wholly inadequate and primitive Blake Field was supplanted by the then pretentious Pratt Field, which was duly dedicated in the spring of 1891. With its going went also the oldtime "cider meets" with their glamor of fun-provoking events, sack races, three-legged races, barrel rolls, backward crawls, plug-hat and consolation races, and occasionally to cap the climax the rough-and-tumble struggle for the possession of a greased pig. As a youngster in common with my Amherst friends I had regarded this occasion as one of the most exciting of the year. Class rivalry was then revealed in its greatest intensity, and we all had our special favorites whom we noisily backed. I do not recall that we were ever invited to sip the cider that flowed from the keg bestowed on the winning class, but I think we did find a way to taste it now and then. From this assorted mixture of track activities developed in due time the more sedate and more closely prescribed program of track events which are commonly accepted as official in this modern and regulated athletic world. Baseball held the center of the stage in the college world of sport. Football, while it had its enthusiasts, did not stir the student body greatly and the manager in my freshman year complained bitterly in a *Student* communi-

cation of the lack of interest. The interest in this sport
grew, however, and by my senior year was strong. Although Amherst had made several enviable records in the
Springfield Intercollegiates, the interest in track was confined largely to the few specialists who performed.

While my mother had wisely decided that I was to live
in college environs during my course, she had felt that for
pecuniary reasons I should board at home. In return for
my board I was assigned the not exactly enviable task of
saying grace at the beginning of the meals. This was not
easy when from fifteen to twenty lively girls were seated
at the tables and dignity was to be maintained. But my
brother before me had weathered the storm, and I dared
hope that I could do as well. It was even reported that he
possessed such rare control that while in the act of saying
grace itself he could cast his eyes about, wink at a respond-
ing eye now and then, and still retain his dignity and composure. For a time all went well. Then one morning, while
I had had no inkling of the plot, the young ladies set out
to put me to the test. At a prearranged signal and while
heads were still reverently bowed all eyes were suddenly
turned in my direction and faces broke into mocking
smiles. I tried my best to outface the congregation and
might have done so had not the fair one at my right just
then stepped on my foot. That was too much and I giggled
outright. My outraged mother terminated the contract at
once, and I promptly joined a group of classmates at one
of the student boarding houses.

The only Convent contact left me after this ignominious
affair was the weekly Sunday night " sing." It was through
no fault of mine that I did not survive this last test. The
young ladies were accustomed to call for their favorite

hymns, for which my mother played the accompaniments. Increasingly the well-known Easter hymn with its repeated alleluias were asked for, and increasingly the " al " in alleluia was held and stressed by those shrill feminine voices. Grins and knowing glances grew also apace until my good mother suddenly discovered what was up. And that ended my last formal contact. From then on such contacts were generally surreptitious and not often under the Convent's sheltering roof.

Naturally the outstanding event of my freshman year was the coming of the new president, Merrill E. Gates. The resignation of President Seelye had left a void which was not at once filled, and the consequent uncertainty doubtless accounted in part at least for the size of the class of Ninety-Four, which was the smallest recorded for some years. The announcement of Gates's election caused no little excitement, as we tried to figure just what kind of a man he was and whether or not he would win our confidence and support. We knew absolutely nothing about him beyond newspaper reports, which were generally fulsomely flattering. When he finally made his appearance, we found him impressive. Tall, handsome, and dignified, with a flowing mustache to accentuate his seeming greatness, he appeared to be a leader we could accept, and this in spite of his first formal appearance at morning chapel when, owing to a slight oversight in dressing for the occasion, he had been promptly nicknamed " Gates Ajar," the title of a well-known book by the popular Elizabeth Stuart Phelps. The discovery that he had promptly installed a tennis court on the grounds behind his house and that he really excelled at that game strengthened our confidence. Yet it was this same tennis court that gave some of us the first inkling that there were weaknesses in this newcomer which boded no good for the future.

Tom Esty and I had won the doubles in the college tennis tournament that year and were early invited to play on the president's court. We had some interesting games, but from the start were a bit puzzled by our opponent's frequent questionings of our decisions as to whether balls which landed on our side of the court were " in " or " out." In deference to authority we graciously yielded at first and admitted that we might have been in error. It became increasingly embarrassing to us as these questions continued. At length came the climax. A serve from the hand of the president himself landed a good two inches beyond the line and was promptly declared " out." Before we realized just what was happening, that august person had leaped the net and with his racquet was pointing to one of dozens of similar spots where balls had hit the gravel, exclaimed excitedly, " I beg your pardon, that ball was ' in ' and here's the mark it made." He had picked out a mark just inside the line, of course, and who were we to dispute the charge. For the moment we ate humble pie, but we declined to play on that famous court again. " Prexy " looked for others to fill our place, but these in turn gradually faded away and for the same reason. Esty and I, at least, were not unprepared for later developments, which are recorded elsewhere.

IV · The Gates Regime

THE ENTHUSIASM WHICH marked the arrival of our new president, Merrill E. Gates, was not to last for long. Just when, or for what specific reasons, the change in the attitude of the undergraduates first took place cannot easily be determined, but it is safe to say that it was a gradual process which gained increasing momentum as the months rolled by. And it was accentuated also by the fact that rumors, increasing in number and significance, reached us that the faculty too were coming to our conclusion that the new president was not of the caliber we had at first believed him to be, and had decided from their own experience that he had pronounced weaknesses of character. The main weakness ascribed to him was at first, and generously, termed " unreliability." Later this was expanded to " dishonest," though a few preferred the more convincing term " liar." Because of my early and friendly contacts as a town boy with many of the faculty, some of these men were willing to extend confidences to me to an unusual, and often embarrassing, degree. And I was a bit startled to have gentle souls like Genung and straight-shooters like Tip Tyler assure me with no little feeling that Gates was chronically dishonest. Not that I was wholly unprepared to recognize the fact, for the early experience which Tom Esty and I had encountered on the president's tennis court had revealed clear evidence of something of the sort, but to hear it from the lips of dignified members of the faculty was something else. And it was all the more startling because our most common contacts with the president were when he presided at morning chapel or occupied the pulpit of the college church. On these occasions he was a fervent Methodist, whose eloquence reached increasing degrees of heat as he talked to God of sin and pleaded for our souls. It was hard to believe that piety of this exalted type could cloak weaknesses which we accepted as parts of our own frail and unformed selves.

It was not, however, only from the chapel desk and the church pulpit that we encountered this outward enthusiasm for the things of the spirit. The mid-week prayer meetings, attended chiefly by members of the faculty, but occasionally by a few zealots from the student body, furnished Gates just the opportunity he most welcomed for turning on the steam, and turn it on he did. The prayers of Tip Tyler and Old Doc on these occasions were famous, but in the newcomer these eloquent and honest saints faced a rival, and even more than a rival, and for probably the first time in their lives found themselves outmatched.

If the few saints among the student body had the privilege of hearing their president at his pious best at the mid-week prayer meetings, the sinners were often forced to hear him under circumstances more intimate but far less welcome, for it was the custom of this would-be guardian of the souls of the students committed to his care to entice the weaker brethren in our midst into the forbidding confines of his office in Walker Hall and there, after having duly admonished them for their shortcomings, force them to get down on their trembling knees and join him in petitions to the Almighty that they might be cleansed from the errors of their ways. And one never knew just when or where the axe might fall. I barely escaped it myself one

morning when I happened to encounter this zealous missionary just in front of Walker Hall. He greeted me with
his famous smile and then, piercing me with his searching
eyes, said with apparent feeling, " Stearns, I never see you
without thinking of your grandfather."

He paused a minute to let the shaft sink home and then
added, " Stearns, I think it would be very helpful to the
morale of the student body if you would rise for the hymn
at morning chapel."

In some consternation I waited for the expected invitation to accompany him to the office on the second floor. It
did not come, but why I never could guess; and my accuser
passed on.

As a matter of fact the rebuke was deserved. In my
senior year my mother had relaxed somewhat the earlier
restrictions governing my contacts with the Convent, and
for pecuniary reasons I took my breakfasts at the family
table just after the young ladies had left the room. We had
moved in my sophomore year from the president's house
to new quarters just beyond the railroad bridge adjoining
Pratt Field, and the trip from the Psi U house, where I
then roomed, to the outskirts of the town and back again
to the college chapel involved not only distance but at the
end the climb up the steep slope south of the campus. My
regular schedule called for departure from the Psi U house
at from five to ten minutes past eight, a sprint, never a
walk, out to the family home where breakfast awaited me,
a breakfast fairly gulped down, and a return sprint up the
breath-taking hill to the chapel, where the exercises began
promptly at eight-thirty. By the time I slumped into my
seat on the last strokes of the bell, I was completely
winded, and as the hymn in question came early on the

program I found it difficult to rise and readily followed the example of at least half of those present who regularly remained slumped in their seats. I really think that in this instance Gates's deserved rebuke did some good, for my conscience was stirred a little and from then on the hymn brought me oftener to my feet.

But it was not only at his office that we encountered the evidences of our president's zeal for our spiritual welfare. Those who were first invited to his home and family table brought back disturbing tales of a program which was truly frightening. Instead of the customary grace offered before the meal, each one present was required, while heads were bowed, to recite a verse of Scripture. We were sure that even if we knew one it would vanish from our minds under pressure like that. We heard all kinds of yarns of what had happened to those who had faced the test. The best, perhaps, was told by Ben Hyde, whose father was then a trustee of the college, and who in consequence had received one of the first invitations to dine at the president's house. According to Ben, who was far from being a student of the Scriptures, when his turn came he could think of only one verse and in a panic he let it go. And it was this, " Thou preparest a table before me in the presence of mine enemies." Where a good story was concerned, Ben had never been noted for accuracy, and so we had our doubts as to the truth of this one. Ben stuck to his version, however, and insisted that since the invitation had never been repeated no further proof of his veracity was needed.

My second personal contact with the president was of a very different character from the " grandfather " episode. It was irritating at the time, but it had a humorous touch as well, and fortunately the humor involved long outlasted the irritation, for in a sense it put Prexy " on the spot," and nothing could have ministered more to our glee than to do just that.

Gates had a wholesome interest in athletics and was a regular attendant at the college games. He was something of an athlete himself, an excellent tennis player in fact. So my athletic activities did not worry him, but social activities, especially where dancing was involved, suggested the lurking presence of the Devil. In my junior year I had been elected chairman of the Junior Prom Committee, and though I had no suspicion of it at the time this dubious honor, to the president's way of thinking, gave clear evidence that I was slipping morally. Two weeks before the prom was to be held I was startled by a summons to the president's office. The greeting awaiting me gave no inkling of the plot that had been hatched to catch me, and after a friendly chat I was about to withdraw when my host, with a broadening smile and courteous friendliness, surprised me by saying, " Stearns, I want to tell you of a great honor that has come to you. There is an important meeting of religious leaders from our various colleges to be held at Princeton over the coming week-end and the Y. M. C. A. has chosen you to be one of our representatives. Jay Stocking of Ninety-Five is to be the other. All your expenses will be paid and it should prove a very interesting occasion."

The Amherst College Y. M. C. A. of my time was neither a popular nor a flourishing institution, and I had never been a member. Furthermore, it was generally recognized as one of the president's pet tools and completely under his domination. If the Y. M. C. A. had elected me for this dubious distinction, it was evident that the choice was the president's and not that of the undergraduate members. And this was the thought that haunted me as I made my way back to my room and sought to regain my composure. My first impulse was to decline the appointment outright. With the prom only a few days ahead and the work in connection with it piling up, I could not figure how I could possibly absent myself for the two or three days required, keep up with my college work, and attend to all the outside matters that must be looked after to insure the prom's success. And this was just the dilemma which the president had foreseen and in which he had deliberately sought to ensnare me. He was to use me as an example to prove his contention that dances were not in harmony with the spiritual and intellectual aims of the college and that those who took an active part in promoting them were in sore need of salvation. The more I thought the thing over the madder I got, but the more fixed in my determination to prove that the president was wrong.

A meeting of the prom committee was promptly called, and I outlined my predicament and explained my purpose. All were in agreement that the president should not be allowed to get away with it and eagerly promised to take on extra work themselves during my absence. Reinforced with this comforting assurance I awaited nervously the end of the week when with round trip tickets in my hands I sought the New Jersey college. I had sent a letter in advance to one of my old Andover classmates then at Princeton, advising him of my coming and telling him that I counted on sharing his room with him during my stay, but I said nothing of the reasons for the trip. He greeted me on my arrival and as we made our way to his dormitory quarters he ventured, " It's great to have you here, Al, but what under heavens happens to bring you at just this time? "

" Well you see, Robbie," I replied, " the college for some unknown reason decided that it wanted me to represent it at the religious conference you are holding here this week, so here I am."

As he listened my friend's face underwent startling changes of expression and finally became one broad grin as he exclaimed, " But, Al, those meetings were held last week, and the delegates all left for home on Monday."

So that was it, and Prexy, in his eagerness to show me up, had not even taken the trouble to check up on the dates. Anyway, I had a chance to see something of Princeton and to enjoy a good visit with my old friend. He kept his promise not to humiliate me by letting his mates know the real reason for my being there, and I left next day with mixed feelings. I wish I had a picture of Gates and the sheepish expression on his face when I reported what had happened. Needless to say I never made a report to the Y. M. C. A., and Gates wisely decided to leave me alone thereafter. Until the famous Senate row some months later our contacts were few and never close.

If anything was needed to add to the increasing antagonism of the undergraduates towards their president, it was supplied by Gates's open hostility to Professor Garman and his famous course in philosophy. In general the student body were aware in only a hazy sort of way that these two men were at odds and that Gates had no liking for the philosophy professor and had been making things uncomfortable for him. But here again my confidants on the faculty took me behind the scenes and revealed the

nature and intensity of the struggle. An outspoken fundamentalist himself, Gates was horrified at a course which at
times actually undermined the inherited religious tenets
of those who took it. And he was duly shocked at the open
boastings of Garman's pupils that they had found something far more satisfying and inspiring than anything the
college prayer meetings or even church services offered.
Here was the Devil openly at work, not only on the college
campus, but actually in the curriculum itself. So reasoned
the president as he girded himself for the battle.

According to my informants the weapons chosen by
Gates for the conflict were many and subtle. First, he had
demanded from Garman that he be allowed to attend his
classes at such times as he saw fit. The request was
promptly and flatly refused, Garman very properly claim-
ing that no one could fairly estimate the final value of his
work by catching only such fleeting and fragmentary visions of it as irregular attendance at classes would supply.
He was generous enough, however, to suggest that if Gates
would agree to attend classes as the students did and complete the entire course from the beginning, a satisfactory
arrangement might be made. This, of course, was the last
thing the president wished to do. By attending occasional
recitations he could easily pick up bits of heresy here and
there which would strongly support his contention that
Garman was dangerous and his course in philosophy the
Devil's potion. Gates was shrewd enough to know that
students who had at times been upset in their thinking by
specific portions of the work as Garman deliberately led
them through the systems of great philosophers of agnos-
tic leanings had, in the light of the completed course, rele-
gated these men to their proper and subordinate place and

had themselves emerged as clearer thinkers and better Christians, strongly inoculated against the poison that these iconoclasts, by themselves alone, so often spread.

Baffled here, Gates turned to other measures to achieve his purpose. In countless ways he made life miserable for the greatest teacher Amherst has probably ever had, centering his efforts on the attempt to put his would-be victim in a place where in public he would be forced to commit himself to beliefs, or a belief, which would brand him a heretic. Knowing that traps were being constantly laid for him, Garman was wary and refused the bait which was so often dangled before him. In desperation Gates at length brought the matter to the attention of his trustees and practically demanded that Garman be requested to resign. But here too he met with failure.

All his life Garman had been forced to battle against ill health, and the intensity with which he threw himself into the work of his classes taxed his limited strength to the utmost, and often forced him from sheer exhaustion to absent himself from class. The added strain to which Gates's attacks subjected him proved more than he could stand. He was plainly worried and his friends were worried. And these same friends were more than worried, though not wholly surprised, when they learned that Garman had sent his resignation to the trustees. On several occasions Garman had been approached by prominent universities which, recognizing his unusual talents as a teacher, wished to enroll him on their faculties. At the moment the University of Michigan was urging on him the acceptance of its flattering offer, an offer which under the existing conditions he felt that he could not decline. Fortunately for us, and fortunately for Amherst, the trustees had become aware of what was going on, and though some of them at least could not be classed as liberal in their theology, they had sense enough to realize the priceless asset the college possessed in Professor Garman, and stood by him to a man. He was asked to withdraw his resignation, which he did.

If the undergraduates had been fully aware at the time of all that was going on behind the scenes, Prexy would have had an open rebellion on his hands. As it was his hold on the student body had been steadily waning for a long time, and it had already passed the breaking point. If anything were needed to shake it loose entirely, the famous Senate fight in my senior year supplied it. Gates had assured us in our freshman year that since we had both come to Amherst that year he would always have a special interest in the class of Ninety-Four. And he did, but not exactly in the way he had anticipated for before we were graduated he was openly telling his friends that until this favored class should have departed he could not hope to administer the college with any degree of success. More than anything else it was this historic fight and the part played in it by the representatives of my class that accounted for the president's gloom.

The story of the college Senate, an institution founded by the broad-minded President Seelye, has been so often told that I shall touch only on the incidents which involved our class, and which led to the official departure of that famous though much abused institution from the Amherst scene. There were two incidents actually, though only indirectly related, that brought the Senate to its untimely grave.

For some years the Senate had been more or less, and

chiefly more, moribund. Each class regularly elected its senators, choosing as a rule its outstanding scholars, but though meetings were held little of importance occurred, and it is doubtful whether the majority of the undergraduates even knew who these senators were. But in the fall term of our senior year an event occurred which suddenly awakened us to the fact that the Senate was not only alive but actually prepared to do business. On the return trip from Hanover after the football game with our Dartmouth rivals, the Amherst rooters stopped off between trains at Greenfield and proceeded to loot the station restaurant, not only of all food within sight, but of everything else that was not nailed down. Dishes and cutlery disappeared first, to be followed by heavier articles of furniture, until the climax was reached when several enthusiasts attempted to load one of the station baggage trucks onto the waiting train. The whole affair was a beautiful illustration of the extent to which mob spirit will go when once in control. The newspapers seized the opportunity to vent their wrath on " college muckers " in general, and especially on those who claimed Amherst as their college. And the college authorities in turn were fairly swamped by demands from the outraged railroad officials that full restitution be made for the damages suffered.

Here at last was the chance for the Senate to justify its existence, and it met the challenge courageously. Numerous meetings were held and scores of students summoned to testify before that august body as to their part or parts in the unseemly affair. In the end the Senate suspended from the college seven men for periods ranging from three weeks to three months. At first a bit stunned by this unexpected evidence of life in an institution that was believed

to exist in name only, the student body howled its disapproval of the severe penalties inflicted on their mates, but
on more sober second thought decided that the punish-
ments were deserved and that the Senate itself had earned
the gratitude of the college for cleansing its smirched
honor and proving to a doubting world that student government could be made to work. By its vigorous and timely
action the Senate had for the first time, in my undergraduate days at least, earned the respect of the student body
and the approval of the outside world. With this newly
won prestige the Senate found itself, a few months later,
facing its severest and final test, a test it would undoubtedly have met successfully had anyone but Gates occupied the president's chair.

It has always seemed to me a bit unfortunate that the
person involved and the charge against him, since this was
to prove so important a case, should not have been a bit
less drab in hue. Clutia, the victim, was a day student,
and hence not well known among the student body as a
whole. He had never been classed as a scholar, and his
contribution to the life of the college came chiefly through
his skill with the banjo, at that time an important instrument in the college musical clubs. He was a happy-go-
lucky chap, always skating on the thinnest ice so far as
scholarship and attendance at classes were concerned, until
his cuts had piled up beyond the limit allowed and a note
was sent by the faculty to his father announcing his suspension. Clutia, who had long suspected that this might
happen, had kept a wary eye on the home mail and on the
arrival of the document in question promptly extracted it,
tore it up, and turning his back on the college, enjoyed to
the full such diversions as the town alone could offer. As a

day scholar he was able to get away with this for some time, and it was not until the Christmas vacation, when his father happened to meet the president on the street, that the truth came out. When the news reached the faculty the suspension, originally limited to the term only, was promptly extended for the entire year. This really meant expulsion for a senior.

The drastic action of the faculty roused the ire of the Senate, whose members felt, and justly, that under the Senate constitution the case fell clearly within their jurisdiction and not that of the faculty. A protest was promptly lodged with the faculty, a protest which it was believed would be heeded, since this had happened several years before under conditions not wholly dissimilar. But Gates was not president of the college in that earlier and happier period, and the protest now availed nothing, the faculty under Gates's whip sticking to its original position. By this time the whole student body had become excited and united in urging the Senate not to give in. The Senate promptly appointed a special committee to draw up a resolution on the faculty's unsatisfactory reply. A day or two later Eugene Lyman for the special committee presented its reply, in which the Senate vigorously contended that the case fell within its and not the faculty's jurisdiction. The faculty's reply to this appeal varied little from its earlier one. The former position was maintained; and now the whole college was up in arms.

At a special meeting of the senior class a committee was appointed " to consider what action it may be advisable to take in order that the principle of self-government at Amherst may be preserved." In addition to two of the class senators, Eugene Lyman and Edward Capen, the class

proceded to elect Harlan Stone, its president, Howard
Ford, and myself for this somewhat dubious job. Our committee was not long in agreeing that Stone was the one
man to whom we would look for expert guidance. We had
not then visualized him as a future Chief Justice of the
United States, but we had early recognized his ability and
justly regarded him as the brainiest man in the class. We
had elected him class president in our sophomore year,
and if my memory serves me, unanimously; and he continued to hold that position through the course. What
added special significance to our choice, and revealed the
instinctive homage paid by youth to those it recognizes as
its betters, was the fact that Stone had joined the fraternity
at whose hands several other groups had experienced a
raw political deal at the opening of our college careers.
Anyway, Stone had had nothing to do with that as he had
not then entered college. He had the " stuff," and that was
enough. The fact that he had early been nicknamed " Doc "
gave further evidence of our prescience, for that title belonged to the learned only, and the bestowal of it, even
though unattended with pomp and ceremony, was the
nearest an undergraduate body could come to granting
the honorary degree commonly reserved for our elders. In
" Frinkie's " debating classes many of us had faced him on
the platform and gone down to pronounced defeat, and in
Garman's course we had again and again listened spell-
bound to his tilts with that keen-minded teacher. Sparks
fairly flew on these occasions and to the delight of all of us
of more sluggish brains.

It was on " Doc's " insistence that we set out first to
marshal our facts. The opinions of outstanding alumni, of
faculty members whom we trusted, and even of prominent

men outside the Amherst field were sought and carefully weighed. Fortified with the wide support given us we, or better Stone, prepared our devastating reply, protesting that the case should not be closed, that our position was sound and rested squarely on provisions embodied in the constitution of the Senate itself, and generously suggesting that if necessary we would accept arbitration. The reply of the faculty to this latest communication was ingenious at least. It was formally addressed neither to the Senate nor to the senior committee, but to the "Student members" of the former; and it intimated that they could not have acted within the constitution because no faculty representatives were included in the names of the signers.

We were still unwilling to give up the fight, and the student senators thereupon voted 8 to 5 to ask the faculty for a joint conference. To this the faculty answered with expressions of appreciation of our offer, but insisted that should such a conference be held, it must be with the definite understanding that the particular case under discussion up to that time would be regarded as closed. That proved too much for any of us to stomach. A college mass meeting was at once called, and the report of the special committee presented. Rice for the committee offered a resolution to the effect that the report as read be adopted, that the student body record itself as having faith in the Senate idea but not in the interpretation given it by the faculty, and that the several classes be requested to ask for the resignation of their respective senators. By an almost unanimous vote this resolution was adopted. Immediately following this stormy meeting, the classes met and formally accepted the resignations of their senators.

So ended the career of a potentially great institution, the creation of a great and broad-minded scholar, the victim of an egotistical and narrow-minded fundamentalist. Several attempts to revive the institution were later made, but the undergraduates rightly were suspicious and had good reasons for believing that if restored the Senate would be stripped of the chief powers that had formerly been delegated to the students, and that in any case it would be so constituted as to be a tool in the hands of the faculty, and especially the president; hence they rejected the proposal.

With scarcely a dissenting voice the students agreed that it was Gates rather than the faculty who was responsible for the Senate's downfall; and they were further and strongly of the opinion that Prexy had seized upon the Clutia incident for the express purpose of doing away with an institution he did not like and which he felt was a definite curb on his own autocratic powers. And this belief became a conviction as various members of the faculty expressed to individuals their full sympathy with our position and their deep regret that the steps taken had proved necessary. To this day, however, I have never been able to figure out just why these zealots for student government failed to put up a real fight against the president and the mere handful of supporters he counted on from their number. Garman, Genung, Morse and others were gentle souls and not of the fighting kind, but Tip Tyler, Frink and a few more did not lack in good red blood. Only a few months before the storm broke, but when the muttering of its thunder could be heard in the distance, Tip had come up to my room one night and for a good half hour had paced the floor extolling the virtues of the Senate and vowing vengeance on any or all who might allow it to die. Finally he leaned over my chair and shaking his fist at me fairly yelled, " Al, if you fellows let the Senate die, I shall hold you personally, you personally," he repeated, " responsible for it." He was in earnest I am sure. All the more I cannot understand why Prexy, for whom by that time few of the faculty had the slightest respect, was so readily allowed to have his way.

As might have been expected the outcome of the Senate struggle intensified to white heat the feeling of the students towards Gates. For the remainder of the college year we lived on the edge of a volcano which constantly threatened to explode. Petty incidents, fairly harmless in themselves but indicating the pressure underneath, cropped up increasingly to warn us of lurking danger and to make life more uncomfortable for Prexy. Some of them were funny, some were mean, and some deliberately insulting. The unofficial alumni yell of Ninety-Four, which some wag had concocted at about this time illustrates what I mean, at least what I mean when I say " insulting," for it certainly was that.

For many years, including the nineties, each class during its senior year was accustomed to produce what was known as its alumni yell, a much more rollicking and expressive jingle than the more staid official class yell so commonly heard in later years at class reunions. The underlying theme of these unexpurgated expressions of joys still to be realized generally centered around conspicuous events or persons that the class had reason to remember. So ours naturally enough centered on Prexy Gates. And this was it:

Hi, Prexy, Hi,
We know you're a sham,
But we don't give a Damn,
We're alumni-i, Ninety-Four.

The "Hi's" were long drawn out and the "Prexy" short and snappy, and the complete yell had a real swing and punch to it that added to its effectiveness. It could be heard at almost every hour of the day, and even night, around the campus and around the town as well, but it was probably never more effectively or more often used, especially in the evening hours, than in front of the president's own home. The evening train from Hamp regularly carried a mixed crowd, patrons of the Smith campus and of Rahar's alike, whose spirits and voices were keyed up enough by the stimulants offered across the river to encourage an outpouring of both, and the lure which the pretentious mansion offered just at the crest of the hill was hard to resist. Invariably a group would fall behind the crowd and the yell would be given with uncommon zest. The echo would be mixed with the sound of scurrying feet as the perpetrators raced through the shadows to their rooms, realizing that if once detected by the insulted president they might well be something else than "alumni" in the end. We had no copyright on this popular production and its use in consequence was not strictly limited to members of our class.

As the feeling against Gates increased in college circles, it seeped out into the town itself, and while the citizens as a rule resorted to no noisy demonstrations of disapproval, they became more and more distrustful and accepted gleefully any opportunity that presented itself to irritate him. One incident especially caused widespread mirth and for several weeks was the talk of the town. A local tailor had made the president a pair of trousers — or should I say pants. Anyway, he called them pants on the bill he sent to the purchaser. In due season he received a check enclosed with the bill rendered, but on the bill the president had crossed out the word " pants " and substituted " trousers." The tailor promptly crossed out the " trousers " and again wrote in " pants," receipted the bill, and added a footnote reading: " Anything over ten dollars is trousers, under ten dollars is pants." Whether he lost a customer by this touch of somewhat fresh humor is not recorded.

Unfortunately the Gates regime did not end with the departure of the class of Ninety-Four from the Amherst campus. Gates still entertained the hope that once we were out of the way he would find smoother sailing, and the trustees evidently were not then quite prepared to take drastic action. He lingered on for several more years, but he had completely lost his grip on students and faculty alike, and his final departure uncovered few mourners.

V · The Faculty

So far as most of the students of my time were concerned, members of the faculty were simply teachers and professors. To me fortunately, and because of my earlier residence in the town, most of them were human, and a number of them good friends as well. The undergraduates saw these men only in their class-rooms or at morning chapel, where on stated occasions individuals from the group presided for a week each, while a select few, and very few, appeared in the seats especially reserved for faculty members. The attention and general conduct of the students themselves were determined very largely by the character of the professor who happened to preside. When Prexy was in the chair, as I have elsewhere indicated, the attitude of the students was at first respect-ful, a bit later puzzled, and later still almost insulting. Old Doc amused us. When he lifted his eyes to the ceiling and pointed his beard in our direction, as he regularly did in his prayers, eyes instinctively were opened if they had been shut and turned in his direction. He entertained us immensely, though he never lost our affection.

Davy Todd, when his turn came, plodded mechanically through the service, making it clear enough to all that he would be glad to be rid of it. There were a number of others for whom our respect was sufficient to assure at least a dignified service.

After handling chapel myself as headmaster for thirty years and looking back on those college days, I am fully convinced that the outcry against academic chapel services was chiefly due to the slipshod way they were conducted. It is perfectly clear that not all members of the faculty are qualified to conduct services of this peculiar kind. It is equally clear that when the right ones are chosen, the response from the student body is heartening.

When a college professor tells his class, as I have known some to do, that he has been assigned to conduct the chapel services the following week, that he dislikes them as much as they do, and cravenly asks them to deal kindly with him, the results to be expected, and the results which actually occur, need no further discussion.

In spite of the trials through which I had passed in the Greek course with Professor Elwell, I still had enough interest in that subject to elect it for my sophomore year. That, however, proved enough, for we had the misfortune to encounter a newly acquired member of the Amherst faculty, Professor Henry Gibbons, commonly known as " Gibby." He, in turn, had the misfortune to be assigned to the classroom directly over the chemical laboratory in old Williston Hall. The combination did not work, at least to the benefit of the Greek course. Gibby's course, even in prep school days, would have been regarded as silly, dealing as it did entirely with grammar, derivations, constructions, etc., with no regard whatever for the character and deeper values which the text contained. I know we were supposed to be reading some of the great Greek authors, but I could never recall just who they were. I do know that in the case of one famous Greek poem of some 1500 lines we had not reached, in our recitation, the two hundredth line when the course ended; yet all had been assigned. Naturally, when we discovered what was happening, the new assignments were never studied in advance.

All of this time we had devoted each day's recitation to analyses of perhaps five or six lines, with constant bickerings over roots and derivations involved. It was a drab and dreary procedure, enlivened here and there by the suffocating odors which filled the room as some daring protester mixed up combinations in the laboratory below that sent reeking fumes all through the building and forced our exit for the day.

At the close of the course all but a few overcautious souls were in a panic, for Gibby had announced that the exam just ahead would cover the entire poem, which we were presumed to have studied. In desperation, we sought to uncover among sophomores who had taken the course during the previous year, Gibby's first year at the college, a copy of the examination given at that time. Our only hope was that we could get some idea of the general nature of the examination before us and could study up a few passages here and there which would fit into the picture and perhaps help us out when the test came. Even so, we expected disaster, and when we sat down in our places and were handed the examination papers, we discovered to our amazement that the paper was an exact duplicate of the one which had been set the previous year. Those of us who had been fortunate enough to look it over were able to pass the course with high marks. Many others were not so fortunate, though I believe Gibby, for some reason, let most of them through. Although there was no cribbing involved in the incident, we all felt pretty sheepish about it, and though not for this reason alone, decided that we would have nothing more to do with this particular course or its supposed teacher.

The following year, with some prompt prodding on the

part of the Amherst Trustees, Gibby accepted a position offered by a prominent university. Before the year was over he was burned in effigy by the irate student body. Evidently we had not fully misjudged him, though our burning was limited to the fumes from the chemical laboratory.

Of all the classes that were real jokes, Montague's French class topped the list. It was supposed to be the snap course of the college, and consequently gathered in all the loafers. Furthermore, it was a semi-elective course, and hence not limited to one special class. The loafers were joined by members of different athletic squads, who definitely chose the course in order that they might have one easy subject on their schedules to offset the time lost in athletic activities. It was in this latter group that I found myself, though I must admit that having had two years of French in my preparatory school, I had a natural inclination to increase my knowledge of that subject. To top it off, the class was scheduled for the two o'clock recitation period, and any class that follows the dinner hour is bound to be in for a certain amount of trouble. "Monty" was small of stature and not exactly large in other respects. He had a fair command of French, but absolutely no ability to impart it. He was what students everywhere would call an "easy mark," and that class, or better the group that gathered in his room for supposed intellectual stimulus, was little less than a circus.

One of our first stunts was to bribe the maple sugar man, "Old Unk" as he was commonly known, to sing under Monty's window. Old Unk wandered down from the Pelham Hills every spring when the sap was running, to

peddle maple sugar around the campus. He must have
been well over eighty years old, and his stooping figure,
with its long white beard well besprinkled with streaks of
brown tobacco juice, and the tin pail from which he extracted with the dirtiest of hands the much sought for
maple sugar, were a common sight on the campus. He also
boasted that he once sang in the Pelham church choir, and
if sufficiently prodded, would respond by squeaking in a
quavery voice something which he called "Home, Sweet
Home," and which, with real effort, might be recognized
as such. It did not take a heavy bribe to persuade this
avaricious countryman to do our bidding. The recitation
would be hardly well under way before the quavering
notes of "Home, Sweet Home" could be heard just outside the window. A member of the group whom we will
call Jones would promptly rise to his feet, and waving his
hand in Monty's direction, would say, "Excuse me, professor, but I will go out and tell the old man to quit singing." Before the echo of Jones's footsteps down the hall
ceased, someone else would rise and announce that he was
going out to find Jones, who had stayed away too long.
So it would go on until perhaps six or eight of the class had
left the room. Monty, through it all, rapping wildly but in
vain for order.

A favorite pastime in my particular class was to eject
Mortimer Schiff from the room. Schiff was probably the
only serious student in the group, and his recitations,
whenever he was allowed to finish them, were all that
could be asked for. Scarcely ever though was he allowed
to finish. A wag named Bishop, who sat near Monty at the
front of the class, would rise in his seat as Schiff got well
under way, beckon sedately to two or three fellows around

the room who would also rise in their places, and then while Monty continued to pound the desk and call for order, the group would make their way to their victim, pick him up in their arms, carry him to the door and deposit him outside, returning quietly to their seats, while Schiff, when he had had time to gather his breath, would sneak back to his place.

Perhaps the favorite pastime of all, however, was to nail Monty to the wall. That needs a word of explanation. Monty's desk stood on a platform, raised about six inches from the floor, and faced the class. The room was small and overcrowded at best. Those sitting on the front benches found it almost necessary to rest their feet on the platform before them. Without stretching their legs to their full extent, the soles of their feet could be brought in direct contact with the desk behind which our victim sat. Half a dozen feet would rest gently against the desk and at a given signal each foot brought enough pressure to bear on that article to send it back a fraction of an inch. This process would be repeated until Monty would suddenly discover that he was sitting too close to his desk for comfort and would move his chair back. The desk would follow him slowly under the same impetus and again the chair with the professor in it would move back, and at about the time the class was ready to adjourn Monty would be pinned solidly between the desk and the wall and the curious group that waited outside the door would see him climb over the desk to extricate himself from the trap. Why he never caught on to the trick perpetrated on him, I can't imagine, but we continued to use it till the end of the course.

Monty's class may have been a joke, but his examinations and make-ups were anything but that, and as each term drew near its close, evidences of distress and panic appeared on many faces. His exams were tough and his make-ups exacting. Excess cuts carried over from chapel and church were regularly distributed among the various courses in alphabetical order, and as French stood close to the top of the list, Monty was sure to find a generous number added to those he had himself recorded. The majority of the faculty were disposed to be lenient in handling these intruders, but not so this eminent French professor. To him a cut was a cut whatever its source, and he exacted the full penalty. As vacations started many a member of that famous class found himself still in the clutches of the man he had humiliated, while his more fortunate classmates were heading for the railroad station or already on the way to their homes. Like Monty himself, when his desk was slowly being forced back against the wall, we were too obtuse to catch on and guard in advance against the impending and ever recurring catastrophe.

Like the French professor Davy Todd was forced to meet his class in astronomy in the early afternoon when the soporific effects of the hearty noon meal had not had time to wear off. Unlike the former, however, Davy was recognized as a friendly soul who took a live interest in our athletic and social activities, and this was enough to exempt him from the indignities so freely heaped on his less fortunate colleague. Furthermore he knew his subject, though he had little interest in attempting to impart his knowledge to the generally uninterested group of undergraduates who composed his class. His interest lay in research, especially the study of eclipses. In that line he was an expert, and the few who specialized in the subject and worked with him at the observatory found him immensely stimulating, and his enthusiasm for his subject contagious. But the formal class itself was a somewhat dreary affair, and those who composed it divided their time between naps and generally unsuccessful attempts to recite.

So much has been written about Old Doc and his historic gym classes that the attempt to record my own experiences would be superfluous to say the least. Yet Amherst College of my day would not have been the Amherst I knew and loved if it had not included that unusual man and the boisterous group of howling dervishes which passed for a class. How far dumbbells and Indian clubs contributed to our physical development I can only guess, but at least our muscles, throat, and lungs as well as body, arms, and legs, were in vigorous action during that brief half-hour. And the period was generally extended of our own volition, while a good proportion of the class, whenever we could persuade the pianist to do his bit, cavorted over the floor in waltzes and two-steps, the favorite dances of the day. Old Doc himself encouraged these extra-curricular activities and smiled benignly on us up to the point where it was time to begin the formal exercises or another class was due. Then his expression changed, the smile disappeared outwardly at least, and his shouts for order, accompanied by the banging of his record book on the palms of his calloused hands, slowly assured us that he was Old Doc indeed and still in command.

After dealing with youth for many years I find myself still a bit awed as I try to figure out the limits of patience and good nature which characterized this beloved man. The smile which I have just said disappeared " outwardly "

on so many occasions when his patience had been tried
to the breaking point seems only to have stolen within,
and not for long at that. Even in his most passionate out-
bursts of protest he still called us " gentlemen," which at
the moment at least we certainly were not; and we knew,
for we had seen the miracle happen daily, that the next
moment that tense face would be wreathed in the old and
familiar smile. With all our horseplay we never lost our
affection for the one we so sorely tried, and inwardly we
had the feeling that behind those forbidding looks there
always lurked a strain of youth which refused to grow old.

The careful measurements and physical tests to which
Old Doc subjected us at the beginning and ending of each
year, and which were duly recorded, amused and puzzled
us. None of us realized their significance or even dimly
grasped the fact that we were serving as guinea pigs in an
experiment which was later to become common practice
in all our colleges, and which was to make Dr. Hitchcock
justly famous as the far-sighted pioneer in this important
field in physical education. The significance of it all was
brought home to me some years later when I was making
one of my periodic visits with Bob Landis at his home, just
outside of Philadelphia.

" I want to show you something, Al," said my host, as
we were rising from our noon meal. He led me into the
adjoining room and took down from the mantel a small
bronze figure, a replica of a famous statue of the " perfect "
physical genus homo, the work of Tait McKenzie, the
well-known sculptor and then head of the physical education department of the University of Pennsylvania. " You
and I are in that," remarked my host, as he turned the
figure gingerly in his hands. " You know," he added, " Mc-

Kenzie decided to cast a figure based on the most reliable measurements he could secure that would represent as accurately as possible what a human figure should be at its best. He sought far and wide for the measurements needed and found that those of Old Doc were practically the only ones in existence that covered a sufficient amount of time to make them of value. So this figure of the ideal physical man is based largely on those Amherst measurements which include yours and mine."

Yes, Old Doc had pointed the way, and the directors of physical education throughout the country were not slow to follow his lead and pay him the tributes he so justly deserved. By his vision and dogged persistence and in the face of amused and sometimes vigorous criticisms, he had won fame for himself and added prestige for Amherst College. We who knew and loved him still take satisfaction in the fact that these honors were bestowed on that unusual and friendly soul who played such a vital part in the Amherst of our time.

To this day I regret that I missed two courses which were among the best that the college offered, John Tyler's biology and Emerson's geology and mineralogy. The former came at an hour that conflicted with another course that I felt to be essential, and the latter was shunned because of my stupid acceptance of a rumor then prevalent that "Emmie" was "down on" athletes in general and regularly scheduled his trips of exploration at hours that conflicted with those reserved for games and practice. All too late I discovered my mistake. In his particular field Professor Emerson stood at the very top, but from the undergraduates' point of view he was a bit austere and too reserved to encourage friendly intimacy. Tyler was the reverse, and his genial, happy-go-lucky ways endeared him to all. That he not infrequently left his classroom to sneak into the basement of the chapel near by to enjoy a cigarette, when cigarettes were comparatively rare articles, in no way lessened his general popularity. His standards for the students in scholarship and conduct were high, but he was human and we liked him.

In history and political economy Amherst had two outstanding scholars and teachers, Anson D. Morse and John Bates Clark. In many ways these two men resembled each other. Both were men of pronounced character, both had to contend against ill health, and both inspired in their pupils a feeling akin to reverence. They were gentle souls but exacting teachers, who knew their subjects and did their best to impart some of their knowledge to us. Our respect for Morse did not prevent us from raiding his unusual orchard now and then, when pears and grapes were in their prime and hung temptingly over the fences on Orchard Street and Northampton Road. That was as far as we ever took liberties with him. Many of his pupils, the late Dwight Morrow included, found in him for years after their graduation a sterling friend and wise counsellor.

I still have in my possession, and typed, the notes taken in Morse's history course. Three of us, Ben Hyde, Harry Whitcomb, and myself worked out a combination which proved of value to us all. " Whit " was the proud possessor of a typewriter, and it was agreed that Ben and I were alternately to take the notes while Whit was to type three copies of each set. A year or two later, when I was serving my apprenticeship as a teacher at the Hill School in Pottstown, Pennsylvania, I had occasion to sense something of the real worth of Morse's work. My old playmate of the early Amherst days, "Billy" Graves, had joined the school's teaching staff for a year. Graves, a remarkably able and versatile fellow, had then thought of making teaching his career and had entered the Harvard Graduate School, where he specialized in history. Owing to the illness of his father, he had accepted the temporary position at The Hill in order to earn some money to help defray his father's hospital bills. After hearing me speak enthusiastically of Morse's history course, he asked permission to look over my notes. When he returned them later he remarked, "That man Morse must be an unusual teacher. Those notes of his are better than anything that I've encountered in my history courses at either Yale or Harvard, and at Harvard I've had their top men in the subject."

Unfortunately for Amherst, Professor Clark remained for a short time only. His ability as a teacher in a subject just then coming into prominence in college curricula was speedily recognized in academic circles, and a call to an important position in Columbia University could not well be resisted. In his withdrawal Amherst suffered a serious loss.

For pure unadulterated friendliness no member of the faculty excelled John F. Genung, listed as professor of rhetoric. A poet and musician combined, "Nungy," as he was affectionately known, was wholly devoid of the eccentricities so commonly associated with both. His smile, which seldom left him, radiated the happy disposition that was his and prompted him to whistle or hum as he walked the streets or went about his daily tasks. He knew his subject and loved his work, but he was not a driving teacher and his classes were somewhat sleepy affairs, though constantly enlightened by his flashes of humor directed at individuals who by their bungling efforts made themselves easy marks for his shafts. The compositions which we were obliged to prepare and hand in supplied him with many an oportunity to drive these shafts home. Too often these effusions represented "joint" rather than individual effort, though signed by those who were supposed to have produced them. I am sure that Nungy was seldom fooled, but his rebukes were mild and left no hurt.

I well recall one of these incidents in which I was involved. My roommate and I were often accustomed to work out our themes together, which generally meant that one of us, who at the moment had the most time at his disposal, did most of the work. In this instance one of us had copied with little change a theme just finished by the other describing the view from the college tower. It was Nungy's custom to pick out several of the best themes handed in and read them before the class, calling for such criticisms as might be offered. On this occasion he proceeded to read the composition on the view from the college tower. Both my roommate and I stiffened a bit with pride as we recognized our handiwork. About half way through the theme, and after he had intoned a flowery description of the Connecticut River "winding like a silver thread in the distance," Nungy slowly put down the paper and took up another. "Here's an interesting paper too," he commented and proceeded to read. It did not take the class long, nor the authors either, to recognize the duplication and snickers filled the room. Completing the passage about the Connecticut River, Nungy laid down the paper and remarked quietly, "I think we have heard this before. And by the way," he added to drive the lesson home, "has anyone here ever been able to see the Connecticut River from the college tower? I haven't." Two rosy-faced youths slumped in their seats and left the class when the hour was over to face the hectic banterings of their mates.

Genung's fame was not limited to the Amherst campus. His books on rhetoric were in common use in schools throughout the country, and he had published articles and even books on Tennyson, Browning, and the Book of Job, poems that especially appealed to him and of which he was a constant student. For some years he conducted in one of the largest churches of Boston a class in the study of the Book of Job, a class made up of prominent business and professional men, and he was frequently called upon to lecture on these and similar themes.

Undergraduates who were musically inclined haunted Nungy's home, where they were privileged to listen to or actually play in the orchestra which he had formed and in which he himself took a leading part. Embryo poets never tired of sitting at his feet as he discussed the poems of Tennyson and Browning, and if, as sometimes happened, they were invited to pick up a lunch and roam with him over the Pelham Hills, the memory of those outings, and especially of stops by the side of mountain brooks to eat their lunches and listen, to the accompaniment of running waters, while Nungy, with free rein and many happy quotations, expounded the merits of the poets he loved, remained with them as a possession forever. For Nungy Amherst College was a shrine. No one better than he felt its pulsebeats and sensed the underlying values and indescribable something which gripped the hearts of the undergraduates and held their affection through their lives.

The songs that he wrote and which even in this later day are so much a part of Amherst life bear clear witness to this.

In Latin Amherst was fortunate in having two outstanding men, Edward Crowell and William, or " Billy," Cowles. The former had passed his prime in my day, but his reputation was known to all and was secure. His heroic courage in his late years when blindness had stricken him and he had to be led to and from his classes, where with memory alone for his textbook he brought home to his pupils the beauties of the great Latin authors, won the respect and admiration of us all.

As for Cowles I doubt whether he was ever appreciated as much as he deserved to be. His inherent modesty was largely to blame. To those of us who enjoyed and profited by his work in class he was justly rated as one of the best teachers we met. His enthusiasm for his subject was boundless and contagious, so much so that it prompted me at least to include Latin on my schedule throughout my college course. The work which we did with him in senior year, which consisted chiefly of sight reading, was a constant delight. Except for the course with Garman, I believe that Billy Cowles's course was the only one in which I never exhausted my allowed quota of cuts. If we undergraduates who knew him best had been asked to name that member of the faculty who most nearly approached our ideal of what a true gentleman should be, I am pretty sure that a majority would have named Billy Cowles.

Of the new men who were added to the faculty during my college course Edwin A. Grosvenor was to win a position and a somewhat nebulous fame that marked him as a bit different from his older colleagues. He joined us at the beginning of my sophomore year, and while I never had occasion to meet him in his classroom, I did meet him elsewhere, and in one instance at least under embarrassing conditions. He began his Amherst career as an instructor in history, switched the next year to French and literature, and still later to modern government. It was in this last position soon after my own graduation that his classroom technique became the joy of loafers and wags and won him an enduring, if somewhat questionable fame.

" Grovey " was definitely a gentleman and a scholar. But he was also in some respects a " sophomore," and especially in his interest in the fraternity, Psi Upsilon, to which he happened to belong. He was a frequent attendant at the meetings of the local chapter and rarely missed those of the national organization. When in due time he was elected president of this latter body, his pride and enthusiasm excelled those of a newly pledged freshman. He gave us all the impression that no higher honor could come to a man than that bestowed on him, and he lost no opportunity to emphasize this truth in our presence. No undergraduate even was prepared to go so far as this, and we were more amused than impressed, when not exactly bored, by these sophomoric lapses on the part of a scholarly member of the faculty. This fraternity obsession was destined to make trouble for me in my senior year.

It fell to my lot to serve as chairman of the rushing committee of the local chapter of Psi Upsilon, charged with the special task of picking a delegation from the incoming class of Ninety-Seven. Our task that year was immensely complicated by the fact that in this group were included no less than seven direct " legacies," normally destined to become good Psi U's; and to make matters worse, five were sons of members of the faculty, and three of them claimed Professor Grosvenor as their father. The Psi U brethren were clear enough in their own minds as to the relative merits and demerits of these candidates, but the pressure put on us from alumni and higher sources was so great and constant that we had to give practically all our time and thought to the legacies alone, while other fraternities picked up men whom we would have been glad to enroll under normal conditions. Eventually we compromised by pledging Edwin Grosvenor, the oldest of the Grosvenor trio, turning thumbs down on the younger twins. Grovey was wild when he learned of our action, dropped all contacts with the local chapter and those who composed it, and knowing who the members of the committee were who had perpetrated the dastardly deed, declined to speak to or recognize us on the street from that day forth. His wrath was somewhat appeased the following year when a more subservient rushing committee admitted the twins to their sophomore delegation.

Of the new men who joined the faculty in the early nineties some were not long with us while a few stayed to become in later years Amherst's " Grand Old Men." Of the former Burroughs and Tuttle in turn struggled with the impossible task of serving as college pastors and doing most of the preaching at the college church. Each in turn gave it up and moved on. Hiram Seelye, or " Little Doc," as he speedily came to be known, joined the physical education department and helped lift the load from Old Doc's shoulders. His wife had the gift of selecting unusually pretty girls for her house guests, and the " fussers " of the undergraduate body were in consequence drawn as if by magnets to the Seelye home when these house parties were scheduled. Nelligan too was added to Old Doc's staff, devoting most of his time to the training and coaching of the college track team. " Tute " Pierce returned to the college for a year as Walker Instructor in Mathematics, and later joined the faculty of Smith College. He tried to teach us geometry, but gained his chief popularity from his special method of handling the excess chapel cuts automatically thrust on his attendance record. " Go home, read a chapter in the Bible, sing a hymn, and we'll call it square," was the formula he regularly announced. " Tute " was not unpopular.

There were several other men on the faculty who could be called good but not great. Richardson in German and Neill in English literature were found stimulating by those who, because of special interest in their subjects, elected these courses, but they made no outstanding appeal to the undergraduate body as a whole. This was in a sense true also of Professor William Esty, though probably his subject, mathematics, in which he was a master, was chiefly responsible for this lack of lure. In chemistry Elijah Harris, " Derwall " to all of us, was undoubtedly one of the outstanding experts in his subject of the time, but his curious manner of speech, interspersed with " em's " and " aw's " and " let me see's," made it difficult for the average student in his class to follow or understand him. Those who excelled in the subject, however, and especially those who worked under his direction in the laboratory, found him immensely stimulating and later joined in large numbers the ranks of America's leading chemists.

With all his faults Prexy Gates did Amherst a great service in selecting for his faculty several exceptional teachers who were to make their work at Amherst permanent careers and to add greatly to the prestige of the college. Arthur Kimball, who faced the task of building up a sadly deficient department of physics, was one of these. Personally I never appreciated his true worth, since the higher mathematics required in that subject was a bit too high for my unmathematical brain. Amherst seems to have had more than its fair quota of semi-invalids on its faculty in my time, for Kimball, like Morse, Clark, and Garman was forced to contend against ill health all his life. Kimball and Clark lived in houses adjoining ours when the family had moved from the president's house to the new settlement just coming into being beyond the railroad cut near Baker's Grove, and they proved delightful neighbors and valued friends.

In persuading George Olds to come to Amherst, President Gates of course made his finest contribution to the college. As " Georgie " was a newcomer, our class did not begin to appreciate the sterling qualities which became so well known to all in later years and stamped him as the peerless teacher, administrator, and man, who won and held the affection and esteem of his colleagues and pupils alike and to an extent not equaled perhaps by any member of the Amherst faculty in recent decades. We recognized him as a square shooter, an excellent instructor, and a friendly soul, who seemed to understand and sympathize with our undergraduate interests. As such he won our confidence, but it remained for those of later years to know him at his mature best and to bestow on him the honors that were so justly his. The editors of the *Olio* from the class of Ninety-Five, who had had two years in which to size up the newcomer, summed up well in their leading article the impression Georgie had already made on the student body. In their closing paragraph they had this to say:

Professor Olds is still comparatively a young man, and is just entering upon his life work. His wide and varied experience, his opportunities for study at the strongest centers of intellectual life, his strong will, his Christian courtesy, the fine and contagious enthusiasm that is felt in all his work, and inspires his students, and his reverent outspoken loyalty to Christ, have given to his work at Rochester and at Amherst a force and an influence which are widely recognized and have been felt in the life of many students. Friends of Amherst look with interest and high hope to many years of work here by one whom all honor and love.

How well this " high hope " was justified the later record clearly reveals.

In the early nineties many of the men who had gained prominence, if not fame, as members of the Amherst faculty during my boyhood days had passed from the scene. Several were still living and were familiar figures around the town, though they had either severed their college connections or were loosening their hold in anticipation of early retirement. Two were outstanding men revered by all and justly rated among the greatest of Amherst's Grand Old Men, William S. Tyler, for many years professor of Greek, and Julius H. Seelye, just retiring from the presidency. I have always regretted that it was not my privilege to enjoy the inspiration of Tyler's masterful teaching. I came to college just a bit too late for that and the farcical course, if it could even be called a course, I encountered under Professor Gibbons quenched any desire I might otherwise have had of enlarging my knowledge of Greek.

From my early boyhood days I had always regarded President Seelye as Amherst's number one Grand Old Man; and I think that he was generally so regarded by the citizens of the town. There was something Olympian about him that inspired respect, if not indeed reverence. He was big physically, mentally, and spiritually. For his day he was broad as well, and the fact that he had served with distinction as a congressman in Washington definitely added to his prestige. He was not so constituted as to invite intimacies, though he was friendliness itself to those who knew him best, and since our families were good friends and my oldest sister an especially close friend of Bessie Seelye, the president's oldest daughter, there were frequent occasions when I experienced at first hand his sympathetic interest in my welfare.

My last contact with this great soul is one that I am not likely to forget. Only a few weeks before his death in the spring of 1895, in response to urgent requests of my mother, I called one evening at Seelye's home. He greeted me with the old-time friendliness, but the inroads of the disease from which he suffered in his later years were painfully apparent and it was evident that he had not much longer to live. As I walked from his study to the door, he followed me, and as we stopped for a moment on the threshold, he held out his shaking hand and said with no suggestion of heroics, " Good-bye, Alfred, I shall probably not see you again. I expect to be translated soon." " Translated? " That word haunted me for some days. Just what did he mean? Eventually it dawned on me. It was just the right word, the only one in fact that could properly convey

Seelye's philosophy of life and death. All his life he had lived in a spiritual realm which he could not disassociate wholly from the more earthly life which so commonly marked the boundaries of human thought and action. To him death was not in itself an end to be followed by another life beyond the grave. It was rather a transition, a continuation and an expansion of the spiritual life he had known here on earth and which he had found so real. Yes, translated was the proper word.

VI · Charles E. Garman

THE GARMAN MYTH — HOW often one hears that expression today around the Amherst campus and among the graduates of recent years! It always stirs my ire, and especially when, as so often happens, it falls from the lips of members of the teaching staff or those associated with them. It savors all too much of a type of defence complex developed, unwittingly perhaps, in those who do not like to believe that as teachers they can never hope to touch the heights reached by this peerless teacher of an earlier year, probably the greatest of the many truly great men whom through its long history Amherst College has known as members of its faculty. With graduates of later years this expression can be fairly attributed to ignorance and the natural haze surrounding a story handed down to them from a seemingly distant past. But to those who were privileged to feel themselves the quickening touch and the lasting inspiration of that master teacher, the term myth, whatever its source, arouses justified resentment. To them at least there was nothing mythical in the experience; it was instead the most real thing they encountered in their college course. It is unfortunate that this derogatory term should have gained the ascendancy it has today. And it is no credit to Amherst College that it has done so. The Garman epic would be more to the point.

So much has been written and so much said about Professor Garman and his unusual courses that it would be foolish for me to attempt to enlarge upon it, even if I could.

And yet no attempt to put in writing my personal recollections of college days could, by any stretch of the imagination, be called complete, if I did not include a summary of what actually happened in that course as I knew it and of its effect on the students of my time. Fortunately Garman was at his peak in the nineties, and I doubt whether any class profited by that fact more than did the class of Ninety-Four.

Long before I entered college in the fall of eighteen-ninety the widespread comments on Professor Garman's philosophy course had reached my ears and stirred my interest, for these comments were far different from the common gossip of the campus and town about college courses in general and the men who taught them. Here was something different, something truly exciting, something that even at a distance cast an alluring spell. To be sure the course was known as the hardest of those that the curriculum offered, but if those who had taken it were to be believed, it was one that could not be ignored if an undergraduate expected to become a full-fledged Amherst man. My interest grew to white heat as in my freshman and sophomore years I listened to the exciting discussions of seniors who seemed to find little else in college life to think or talk about. Even athletics and social activities received scant attention in the " bull sessions " staged by upperclassmen at meals, in the fraternity houses, and even on the paths and grounds of the campus itself. An atmosphere of this unusual intensity was bound to have an effect on lowerclassmen, and it was with keen eagerness that we looked forward to the day when we too should become initiates.

Not all of my classmates elected the course in philosophy. A few timid souls, including those who had never overexerted themselves in their scholarly pursuits, were a bit frightened at what they had heard of the exacting demands they were likely to face if they were rash enough to enroll, and so passed it up to their personal loss and, in some cases, to their lasting regret. But the large majority accepted eagerly the challenge, and the group that assembled in Walker Hall on the opening day of our junior year pretty well represented the class as a whole. Some of us were still a bit frightened at our own temerity as we realized what we had done and sensed something of the nature of the pathway that lay before us and on which we dared venture to tread. But the die had been cast.We were game and we were eager. No teacher could have asked of his pupils more than that.

The arrangement of topics and the development of the course itself as Garman had so carefully planned them are well known and need not be dwelt upon. The work of the junior year, chiefly a study of the working and reactions of the mind, with the use of such laboratory equipment as Garman had been able to secure, largely at his personal expense, proved exciting. But the real thrills came in senior year when we wrestled with the problems of philosophy itself and worked our way into and out of the various systems that at different times had held their sway. And those thrills increased steadily as the year progressed, reaching their height in the spring term. No member of that class could have been hired to miss one of those spring term recitation periods, and the few who were occasionally compelled to do so were loud in bemoaning their fate. Trips I had to make with the ball nine that spring, something that under ordinary circumstances I would have looked forward to with eagerness, were begrudgingly accepted as unwarranted intrusions and the thought that they had forced me to lose a recitation or two in philosophy rankled for long afterwards.

The fact that Garman exercised such an unusual influence on his pupils is all the more remarkable in view of his physical condition and the exaggerated means he employed to meet the handicaps which ill health forced upon him. The weaknesses from which he suffered centered at the time largely in his throat, and his voice was weak and a bit rasping in consequence. Due probably to poor circulation he craved abnormal heat, and even in the hottest summer weather his recitation room was if anything a bit hotter than the air outside, all too little of which was allowed to circulate because of the threat of dangerous draughts. However hot the day might be he regularly wore a heavy overcoat supplemented by a silk scarf around his neck. In his home, which we often visited in the evening hours, I doubt whether the thermometer ever registered much lower than eighty degrees. Here were all the idiosyncracies on which undergraduates ordinarily pounce with glee and accept as clear evidence of a teacher's incompetence or worse. Perhaps we laughed about them now and then, but not one of us allowed them to affect by one iota the respect, admiration, and reverence which that gifted and scholarly teacher inspired.

A complete estimate of Garman's personality and the qualities of mind and soul which enabled him to grip so strongly the hearts of his pupils would be a difficult task. There were several, however, recognized by everyone. First of all, I think, was the keenness and brilliancy of his mind. The often-quoted comment of a distinguished member of our class, Chief Justice Harlan F. Stone, well expresses a judgment shared by us all. It was at one of our class reunions and in answer to a query of a cub reporter for the *Amherst Student,* who had asked rather impatiently just what there was about " that man Garman " that excited so widely the graduates of an older generation. Stone's reply to the effect that in all his experience on the bench of the Supreme Court, which had brought him into intimate contact with the keenest minds the country could produce, he had yet to encounter one that he rated equal to that of Garman, should be proof enough that our own high estimate of the quality of that mind was not a biased one. Whatever varied walks of life the rest of us may have followed since college days, I am sure that each and all would agree that the estimate of the Chief Justice represented that which we too, though under more limited conditions, had ourselves formed.

Deeply as the keenness of that mind impressed us, the fact that it could and constantly did center itself on us individually and our personal problems carried still greater weight. Hesitatingly at first, we gathered courage to place before it questionings prompted by the classroom discussions or by our study of the pamphlets which were placed at our disposal, questions which we feared were really trivial and for which we might rightly have found our own answers. But reassurance came at once as those piercing black eyes, which always seemed to turn inward to study if not guide the processes of thought within when a baffling problem was under consideration, assumed the expression we had come to recognize and assured us that trivial as we might deem our problem the fact that it did raise a question was enough to justify the careful attention this master teacher invariably gave it. Seldom though, if ever, did we get a direct answer. More often a revealing illustration or a penetrating query that forced the answer from us was our reward and we were left with the feeling that in some mysterious way that answer was our own.

Next to this brilliancy of mind itself, Garman's grip on his students was due, I think, to the methods he employed in his classroom. In these as in his thinking he was far ahead of his times. He never delivered lectures of the kind common in classroom procedure. He never listened to recitations as such based on textbooks or notes scribbled hastily at earlier gatherings. To be sure he did outline in his pamphlets and in advance the bare substance of what coming recitations were to cover, but these outlines, far from supplying answers, were deliberately intended to stir questionings which not he but we by our heated discussions were to solve for ourselves. And this was equally true when at times he himself asked us to take notes on topics he carefully outlined. His classroom for these reasons differed from any other I attended during my college course. They were actually an open forum where teacher and students alike discussed with vehemence at times the problems that the course as it developed had brought to the fore. I do not mean to say that Garman did not guide us in our debates; but such guidance as he supplied was subtle, never autocratic, and aimed always to force us to raise and answer for ourselves the questions through which we were eventually to see the light. Nothing could have indicated more clearly his unwillingness to produce final answers than the fact that the discussions begun in the classroom never ended there. They were continued through all hours of the day and much of the night wherever groups of his students happened to meet, at fraternity houses, boarding tables, on the campus, and even at times in the early morning hours before breakfast when excited individuals by twos and threes elected to begin the day in adjourned debate.

In this classroom procedure which Garman emphasized I have always felt that he had, whether he realized it or not, a valuable ally in Frink and his course in debating, for Frinkie had taught us from freshman year to think on our feet and to put our thoughts into clear and compelling expression. And it was just this that we did, or tried to do, each day in Garman's classroom. The abler men of the class, notably Stone, Luther Smith, Lyman, Capen, Rice, and perhaps one or two others would probably have been able to do this in any case, but for the rest of us the training in debating proved a wonderful asset. At least we were no longer afraid to argue, even if our arguments could not always be sustained. Indeed we welcomed this larger and more challenging opportunity.

A third factor which undoubtedly contributed greatly to the glamor of the course was the subject itself. Philosophy seemed a pretty hazy and indefinable thing to most of us before we tackled it, but it speedily became something wholly different as Garman made us realize that since it dealt with us as individuals, our inner selves and our relations to our fellows, our place and our responsibilities in a universe governed by law and motivated by purpose, a purpose in the fulfilment of which each one of us is destined to play his part, it was actually the most important subject of all. A great teacher, whatever his special subject, can, if inspired, do all this to a limited degree, but philosophy from its very nature offers the opportunity par excellence. And just because he believed this Garman had earlier chosen philosophy as the best instrument available for the accomplishment of the high purpose to which he had dedicated himself as a teacher. All of this we were made to realize, and the realization stirred increasing interest and effort.

Fourth in order, though by no means in importance, I would put Garman's own personality, so richly spiritual as well as intellectual, and the deep but unobtrusive religious convictions which colored all his work. There was nothing dogmatic in Garman's religious beliefs nor anything platitudinous in his exposition of them. They lay at the very core of his thinking and teaching. Like Seelye before him, Garman lived in a spiritual atmosphere which was a part, indeed the basis itself, of earthly life and that of the universe as well. Like Seelye too Garman might well have said that death involved no end but only a " translation."

It has always seemed to me deeply significant that religion as interpreted by this scholarly teacher was so eagerly accepted by groups of undergraduates who in the majority of cases were in no sense outwardly religious. These same fellows reacted as undergraduates regularly do to formal and orthodox religion as it was presented to them through the customary channels. Church and chapel services interested and helped a few, left others indifferent, and not a few cold. And yet almost without exception these same men found in Garman's teaching something that satisfied an inner hunger and made religion a real and vital part of life itself. Here was something very different from the platitudinous prayers and talks to which they had listened in chapel and the college prayer meetings. This was basic and could not be ignored. Still more, it gave a meaning to life, a meaning to one's place in life and the work required of him, and ideals to be realized by individual effort. In marked contrast man-made dogmas and doctrines seemed only childish and silly.

My own personal experience illustrates in a way what I mean. At the close of my college course I was undecided as to the profession I should choose for my lifework. But, thanks to Garman, I was filled with a desire to be of service in the world, to contribute something if I could to the betterment of my fellow-men and hence to the furthering of what we had come to believe was a universal and divine plan. I had thought of the ministry as a possibility, but concluded that it was too restricted by dogmas, creeds, and customary church procedure to enable one to preach and practice the broader type of religion which the course in philosophy had made so natural and real. After three years of teaching I was persuaded to take, in addition to limited work at Phillips Academy, the regular course offered at Andover Theological Seminary. The seminary still counted some outstanding men on its faculty: George Harris, later to become president of my own college; George Foote Moore, destined to rank in after years as one of Harvard's most brilliant teachers; Charles C. Torrey, who in his maturer years at Yale was rated as America's ranking Hebrew scholar; and several others of recognized ability. I was privileged to sit under these men, and yet after the warmth and breadth of Garman's teaching the Andover experience proved a cold douche. Whatever doubts may have lingered in my mind as to the opportunities offered by the ministry as such were completely dispelled, while opportunities to be found in a school for boys seemed unlimited and basic. Here was the chance to serve, and free from the man-made restrictions imposed by church and creeds. To this larger and challenging field I gladly turned.

The ministry probably lost little by my decision, but I am confident that the narrowing restrictions it imposes have kept and continue to keep out of its ranks many outstanding men of character and high purpose whom it so . sadly needs. Stretched out on the shaded lawn of the Hill School one spring day, two of my fellow teachers and I discussed this problem with deep earnestness. One had ranked among the first three scholars in his class at Yale. The other had been valedictorian of his class at Williams. The former became a distinguished surgeon, destined to enjoy a world-wide reputation. The latter accepted a position with a large manufacturing company and eventually filled the position of its highest executive officer. At the time of our " bull session " all were fresh from college, and all were eager to make their lives count for as much as the world would permit. The chances offered by the ministry were weighed with care but eventually discarded, and all because it was felt that restrictions encountered there would prove too forbidding, too cramping, too likely to tempt if not force a man to be not quite true to his inner self and deepest convictions. Perhaps we were not big enough to realize that these reluctances could and should be overcome. I do not know. What I do know, however, is that our experience has been and still is shared by many able boys just emerging from college gates whom the ministry can ill afford to lose.

Garman's deepest religious feelings found their finest expression in his exposition of theism, something new or at best only vaguely sensed by most of us at the time.

Brought up under the prevailing orthodox atmosphere of our several homes and communities, we still entertained a shadowy notion of God as a Supreme Being far removed from this earth of ours but guiding it by remote control from this nebulous operations center. To think of Him as an all-pervading and living Spirit, of which our individual lives were but an expression, no more to be separated from that Spirit, to use one of Garman's favorite illustrations, than the waves can be separated from the sea of which they are a part, proved a new and tremendously enticing thought. That did give meaning to life, and to our individual life too. For the first time we could grasp the true meaning of St. Paul's oft-quoted saying, " In Him we live and move and have our being."

While it is true that Garman's religion was never expressed in the conventional and platitudinous language to which most of his colleagues were addicted and to which we constantly listened at chapel and church services, it is equally true that this great teacher found the Scriptures an inexhaustible reservoir of apt illustrations for the support of his views and the principles he stressed. These in themselves were enlightening, but they became commanding when they were interspersed with striking illustrations from the latest discoveries of science, in which youth always has such keen and wholesome interest. And it was to science that Garman constantly and enthusiastically turned in support of points he wished to make. We had been led to believe that science and religion could not be reconciled and that the battle between them was on in deadly earnest. Now they had become allies, and that was something different and immensely satisfying. Since that earlier day a half-century ago science has kept us almost breathless with its new and startling discoveries, and yet I am sure that had he lived through this significant period Garman would have welcomed with unfeigned delight each new miracle of science and grasped it eagerly as an added manifestation of the activities of the all-pervading Spirit which we call God.

It is the concrete rather than the abstract which leaves its lasting impress on the plastic mind of youth. Garman recognized this as his constant resort to illustration clearly reveals. And the sources on which he so readily drew knew no bounds. Homely too these illustrations often were, but fraught with new and vivid meaning as he used them. The whistle of a passing locomotive — the sound waves registering on our ear-drums and interpreted by our brains; the brilliant colors of an evening sunset — light waves registering on our eyes and interpreted again by our brains. " The low sun gives the color " — then what glories might not we see if by chance our eyes were differently constructed and capable of registering and passing on to the brain the glare of the noonday sun! The beauty of the rose, the odor of the violet — and all taking on new meanings as we were made to sense what they really are.

It doubtless was a combination of these various factors that cast its spell over that unusual classroom in Walker Hall. Not otherwise can I account for all that happened there, and all that was carried from that room to supply food for thought and constant debate through the rest of our waking hours. We met on the last hour of the morning schedule, and the recitation was supposed to end at twelve-forty-five when the noon meal was served. But the bell announcing that fact and so eagerly welcomed by other classes was hardly noticed by us. We merely sat in our seats and waited. A brief pause, and then from that figure seated behind the desk the oft-repeated announcement, "The bell has rung, gentlemen. I'm perfectly willing to continue the discussion if that is your wish, but no one is required to remain." But remain we did to a man and the arguments continued for fifteen, thirty, and occasionally forty-five additional minutes, while waiting dinners grew cold or irate boarding-house keepers in disgust swept the tables clean, leaving only Deuel's soda-fountain to minister to empty stomachs. But none complained, and still unsatisfied groups in the evening hours would head for Garman's house nearly a mile away to continue the morning's argument.

To those who so glibly speak of the " Garman myth " I am prone to believe that they would well profit by heeding a bit of advice which Garman himself constantly dinned into the ears of his pupils; "Gentlemen, first define your terms."

Garman taught us no special brand of philosophy. He never sought to. But he did teach us to think for ourselves, to weigh and balance, accept or discard as our final judgments dictated, provided only that truth and truth alone should be our ultimate goal. Still further he filled us with a consuming desire to serve and to dedicate our lives and our talents to the making of a better world. His technic and emphasis shifted with the changing times, but his purpose never. If in the earlier years many of his pupils entered the ministry, it was because at that time this particular field seemed to offer the greatest opportunity for the constructive service he advocated. And if, as happened during later years, these pupils were found in larger numbers in other professions, in business and in public life, it was only because the shifting currents in a changing world had enlarged and emphasized the new opportunities in these fields. But whether in the ministry, in business, or in public life the men who were privileged to feel the quickening touch of that inspiring teacher entered upon their chosen tasks with a higher conception of duty and a compelling determination to make their lives count in furthering the fulfilment of an unfolding and divine plan.

VII · *Athletics*

MY AVERSION TO ENROLLING at Amherst College, which I have mentioned in a previous chapter, was strengthened by an experience during the latter part of my Andover course. The Amherst nine appeared on our campus to play a regularly scheduled game. Rumors had reached us that Amherst's team that year could not be called a strictly amateur outfit; and the game had not been long in progress before this truth became apparent to all. Among the recruits gathered in by the Amherst management were two outstanding men, Walbridge and Sexton, who early revealed their unacademic character. I think there was still another, but I have forgotten his name. Walbridge, according to the story, had been a policeman in Providence who, under some inducement evidently, had found his way to Amherst, while Sexton was a rough and quarrelsome chap who later joined one of the professional clubs. The latter transferred to Brown the following year and was promptly elected captain of the varsity nine, a team known to all as having been bought outright and in consequence blacklisted by the more respectable college clubs. The influence of these two men on their mates was anything but uplifting, while spectators were rightly disgusted. Amherst's reputation in the outside world was definitely harmed by this departure from accepted amateur standards.

The redeeming figure in this mixed group was Cornelius J. Sullivan, the captain, known as Sully to everyone at the time and to the countless friends he gathered around him

in later years. I liked him from the time of our first meeting when, since he knew that my leanings were all for
Yale, he went out of his way to extol the virtues of Amherst.

When I first reported as a candidate for the nine in the
winter term of my freshman year, Sully was again captain of the team and assured me that he was counting on
me to fill an infield position. Having torn a ligament in my
shoulder when I was working overtime at the pitching job
at my old school, I was forced to abandon any hopes of
occupying the pitcher's box in college, and was promptly
assigned by Sully to the position of second base.

Sully's enthusiasm was contagious and his love for the
game profound. All of us were inspired by him and worked
our heads off to make his team a winning one. He early
took me under his wing and treated me almost as a brother,
insisting that we should room together on our numerous
trips and extending priorities in many other ways.

Besides being a natural-born player, Sully was an unusual chap, with keen Irish wit and a heart overflowing
with generosity and good-will. He played the game hard
and for all it was worth, but always on the level, voicing in
no uncertain terms his displeasure if and when any of his
mates did anything crooked. Once his friend you were his
friend for life, as I had special reason to testify many years
later.

Shortly before my retirement as headmaster at Andover,
I had suddenly found myself in the Phillips House in Boston where I was destined to undergo a major operation
which kept me under the care of doctors and nurses for
nearly two months. A few days after the operation itself,
when I was presumably on the road to recovery, a little
set-back occurred due to a clot of blood that had decided

to wander around through my anatomy and seemed destined to end its travels at my heart. This, at least, is what the doctors told me later, and I know that for a few hours they were worried and haunted my room to an unusual degree.

I was uncomfortable that night, sleep seemed to be out of the question, and I was counting the hours till daylight when my night nurse appeared at the door. Discovering that I was awake she said, "Two large boxes of flowers have just arrived, but I don't suppose you want to be bothered with them tonight. Perhaps we had better wait until morning." I assured her that daylight and darkness seemed alike to me at the moment and suggested that she bring them in. She did so and I noted as she opened them that they were from the Montgomery Rose Company, located on the outskirts of Amherst on the road to Northampton. Two dozen gorgeous long-stemmed roses appeared from the interior of the boxes and the card which accompanied them was handed me. Cornelius J. Sullivan was the name inscribed on it. That was enough for me. The significance of this tribute of affection and good will came to me at once and for a moment undermined my control. Frankly, it took a little time for me to brush aside the tears that welled up in spite of my best efforts to control them.

On our numerous jaunts back and forth from Northampton in connection with our trips to other colleges, the buses which conveyed the team had regularly passed the old pasture adjoining the present greenhouse of the Montgomery Rose Company, where as a small boy I had earned the first money of my life driving our own and our neighbor's cows to and from their feeding ground. I suppose that on different trips in the later years I had mentioned that fact, boylike, dozens of times. Sully had not forgotten it. He was in New York when I was in the hospital, and I had not seen him for several years. Someone had told him of my condition and whereabouts, and that was enough. Recalling the story of those earlier years and with that overflowing sentiment for which he was always famous, he had telephoned to the greenhouse and asked that the roses be sent to my hospital quarters in Boston. A week or two later he appeared at the hospital room itself and told me that he was shortly to leave for California, where he planned to pass the winter; that his Chinese cook and another servant had gone before him to prepare his cottage, and that he counted on my accompanying him. He added that his car would be at the hospital door to take me to the train, that it would meet me on my return and carry me to my home, and that the whole adventure would not involve the outlay of a single penny on my part. That was Sully at his best. That best was constantly in evidence, as his many friends can testify. Small wonder that those friends were legion.

Perhaps an incident which occurred in a game at Williamstown during either my freshman or sophomore year, I forget which, will illustrate better than anything else the real stuff of which Sully was made. I have a rather hazy recollection of it myself, but it has been confirmed in later years by several Williams men who were then undergraduates and who insist that it actually happened.

It was a very close game and nearing its end. Whoever was ahead at the moment, the chances of final victory were about as good for one side as for the other. An Amherst man was on third base when the Amherst batter hit a "Texas leaguer" out into left field, where the Williams fielder, "Chick" Arthur, as he was known, came tearing in for the fly, dove forward to intercept it if he could before it hit the ground, and came up with the ball in his hand. The umpire promptly ruled that Arthur had trapped the ball and that it actually hit the ground before reaching his glove. Arthur vigorously protested and rushed up to Sully, who was coaching on the third base line, insisting that he had caught the ball fairly and that the umpire was wrong. Sully listened, and then, looking him squarely in the face said, "Honest to God, Chick, did you get the ball before it hit the ground?" "Honest to God, Sully. I caught it." Sully looked him over for a moment and then, as a grin spread over his face, said, "Well, Chick, your word's good enough for me." Turning, he called the Amherst runner from the bench, placed him back in his position at third and surrendered the allowed run. The Amherst bench was on the other side of the field back of first base, while the Williams grandstand ran along the third base line. At the close of the inning, Sully came by the grandstand on his way to the bench. The Williams crowd rose, as one man, and cheered him to the echo for this fine piece of sportsmanship. Sully stood it for a minute and then, his Irish humor getting the best of him, stopped in front of the grandstand, raised his hand and said, "Look here, you Williams fellows, I've got something I want to say." The crowd subsided promptly and Sully, the grin still spreading on his countenance, added, "I want to tell you one thing: Chick Arthur is the *only* man in Williams College whose word I would take." He continued on to his destination and the Williams crowd, stunned for a minute, regained their breath and cheered him louder than ever. I like to believe that the story as I have told it is wholly true, for it was at least typical of the man we had come to know and admire.

Sully had one weakness which amused us all though we said little about it to him. We tried that early, but finding how seriously he took the thing himself, promptly desisted. He was full of superstitions. Suspended from a very delicate chain which he always wore around his neck was a charm, ordinarily concealed beneath his undershirt. Omens of various kinds, which amused us, troubled him seriously. I well recall the day when we were dressing in our Greenfield hotel room for a game that was to be played that afternoon. Carelessly, I had put on my undershirt wrong side out, and noting the mistake, I started to pull it off and make the needed change, when Sully suddenly leaped toward me and the next moment his fingers were fairly pinching my shoulders. He glared at me in evident distress, exclaiming, "Don't do that, Al! Don't you know that's the worst possible luck?" I started to laugh, but he was too serious for that, and I reluctantly let the shirt remain wrong side out. What effect this had on our luck that afternoon was never clear to me.

It was largely under Sully's influence that I started my first summer ball playing. In those days it was customary for the members of New England college teams to invest a good part of their summer vacations playing on what might be called semi-professional nines. Such teams were generally located in towns where baseball interest ran high and rivalries were keen. Under the rulings covering amateurs in the nineties one could play on a team of this kind without losing his status, provided he accepted no reimbursements in the form of actual cash. He could get his expenses and that was all. Some met the test, others did not; and the methods employed to secure pecuniary returns without technically surrendering one's amateur standing were devious and clever. Northampton, Greenfield, and Brattleboro, Vermont, were centers of baseball interest, and it was with teams representing these towns, and chiefly Brattleboro, that Sully and I regularly played. As we declined to play for anything beyond our actual expenses, we were treated as privileged characters and allowed to room and board at the Brooks House, Brattleboro's best hotel, while our team-mates made their headquarters at the less expensive American House down the street. It was on this same team that I found myself playing with Stuart, Amherst's outfielder and slugger of earlier days and my boyhood hero at the time.

Another custom, and a most delightful one, was for the men representing these town teams to shift in early August to the numerous hotels scattered through the White Mountains. The girls who, with their families, patronized these popular summer resorts in those days of limited travel facilities found themselves anchored there for the season. The managements were in a quandary when it came to providing sufficient entertainment because of the lack of members of the sterner sex, and in consequence college men, especially those who could play ball, were in great demand. Not only were we expected to play our games for the entertainment of our fair friends, but we were drafted as well to supply companionship on coach rides and partners for the dances. It was a happy, care-free life and we thoroughly enjoyed it, though I must admit that it furnished little intellectual stimulus.

The memories of those evening coach rides over the

narrow and winding roads of the White Mountains still stay with me, and as I drive my car through these same mountain roads today, I fancy I can hear the echoing notes of our bugler at he announced to the world that we were on the move. The rides generally carried us to and from neighboring hotels and the dances which were held there. Each hotel had its good and bad points. One had the prettiest girls, another the smoothest floor, and another the best food. Some, on the other hand, we qualified as beneath contempt.

The days of all days in the mountains were the annual East and West side Coaching Days held every summer. Coaches came from all over the mountains, and prizes were offered for those which were best decorated, those which came the longest distances, those which carried the prettiest girls, and those which boasted of the finest horses. None appeared with fewer than two pairs of horses. The number often rose to four pairs. Wentworth Hall, where I served for two summers as captain of the nine, could not boast of any surplus of pretty girls or fine horses, but it always made an effort to excel in decorations. On one occasion, we met with no little difficulty in finding suitable and colorful garments for the male members of the party. We had our white flannel trousers, but coats of the right hue were hard to locate. Eventually, we raided the bar-room and decked ourselves with the white coats of the barkeepers, which at a distance matched up well with the gay colors of our young lady companions, but which were so short behind that we did not dare rise from our seats. Anyhow we did not win the prize.

The last game I played in the mountains on Coaching Day at Lancaster, N. H., came very nearly being my last

day on earth. The ninth inning was nearly over. Our opponents were at bat with two men out. A runner who had
reached first attempted to steal second. The ground was
very rough and the throw by Pitt Drew, Dartmouth's famous catcher, a bit wide. I stepped back of the base line
so as to touch the runner from behind. As he dove for the
base, he struck a hump in the ground and his heel, jerked
forward by the sudden stop, caught me on the side of the
face as I was stooping to put the ball on him. That was
the last I knew about the game until two hours later, when
I regained consciousness in a room of a nearby hotel.
My friends tried to console me by assuring me that I had
not dropped the ball and that the runner had been declared
out. My trip over the mountains to Wentworth Hall that
night was a tough one, as I sat on the rear platform of the
car, nursing as best I could an aching head and a badly
upset stomach. For nearly a week after I shunned the hotel
dining-room, since my face had swollen to the size of a
small pumpkin. To this day a semi-numb spot on my cheek
and a slight protrusion of the cheek bone which insists on
getting in the path of my razor blade keep that incident
very much alive.

Intense rivalry between the proprietors of the several
hotels added to the excitement surrounding these contests
and was sometimes responsible for amusing incidents. This
rivalry was especially keen between General Wentworth
and the proprietor of the Intervale House. Both were ardent fans and constantly sought to outwit each other. On
one occasion, in preparation for a Coaching Day game, the
General sent me to Boston with instructions to collect the
best group of college players that could be found, regardless of expense. I did just that, and the Wentworth Hall

nine on the day of the game consisted truly of a star aggregation. During the practice the General came out to our
bench in evident distress. "Stearns," he ventured, "do
those Intervale players look familiar to you?" I admitted
that they did not, and later discovered that the General's
rival had imported for the occasion the Portland professional team, at that time leading the New England League.
But the game had to go on, and we still believed that with
luck we could win. With the aid of an urgent telegram
promising a generous honorarium, I had lured Ted Lewis,
Williams's star pitcher, to make the long journey from out
in New York state to fill the pitcher's box, but to my distress the General insisted that our regular pitcher should
start the game lest his feelings be hurt. Over my vigorous
protest he did, and the Portland players took kindly to his
offerings. Lewis was promptly called in from the bench,
but the game had already been lost. To make matters
worse the General, who had lost his bets and his cash, had
lost also for the time being his earlier generosity and tried
to persuade Lewis to shade the price which he had been
promised for his services. Lewis stuck to his guns and won,
but he never quite got over the insult — for it was little
less than that — and to his dying day, when he was President of New Hampshire State University, loved to josh me
about it whenever we met.

The summer following my sophomore year supplied a
slight change of program so far as I was concerned, for I
was asked to captain a nine the Boston Athletic Association was gathering, composed, except for myself, almost
wholly of Harvard men, to tour the country and play numerous athletic clubs scattered about. For a week we took

on athletic clubs in the vicinity of New York; another week those around Philadelphia, especially two at Atlantic City and Cape May, where the Princeton and University of Pennsylvania nines were holding forth. Then we headed west, meeting the Allegheny Athletic Club at Pittsburgh, a team made up almost wholly of Yale men. From Pittsburgh we made for Cleveland and Detroit, returning by way of Buffalo and encountering in those centers, in the guise of athletic clubs, nines composed chiefly of the representatives of the colleges and universities of their sections. It was an interesting experience, but one which I should not care to repeat.

My mother had been opposed to my making the trip from the start and I had pleaded with her that it offered a rare chance for a country boy like myself to see something of the world, especially in company with such a fine group of college fellows as I had anticipated the Harvard group would prove to be. I had known intimately most of the Yale players at that time, many of whom had been my friends and team-mates at Andover, and one could not have asked for a cleaner and wholesomer lot than they. The men who made up our Amherst team were of the same high class. It was that type of fellow that I expected to chum with during the six weeks that the Boston Athletic Club was to be on the road. But I was doomed to disappointment.

The Harvard nine of that year had made an especially good record and had won the " Big Three " championship by a good margin. Its mainstay was its battery, composed of huge red-faced Jack Highland and its catcher, known as " Slugger " Mason. This battery was to be our mainstay too, though, as we were to play almost every day on the trip, we carried along two extra pitchers, Jack Highland's younger brother and a fellow named Howe. The captain of Harvard's team, Louis A. Frothingham, was one of only three members of the regular nine who passed up the Boston Athletic Association assignment. I could not understand at the time why they did it, but it was for that reason that association officials appointed me captain; "to avoid jealousies" was the way they put it. Later, I discovered that Frothingham and his friends knew too well what was to be revealed to me and had wisely decided to remain at home. With practically two exceptions, Cook, our third baseman, and Miah Murray, an ex-Washington League catcher, the group was about the toughest and roughest crowd I have ever dealt with. The manager was perhaps the worst of all. More than once we were expelled from hotel rooms because of the orgies in which some of this group indulged on their return from "doing" the cities in which we happened to be staying at the time. The manager, a year or two later, committed suicide in some miserable and unsavory mix-up in one of our larger cities. I was constantly forced to assert myself to the utmost to keep these fellows in line while on the field. Outside of that I was helpless and made no attempts to interfere.

Cook, Murray, and I chummed together most of the time, haunting the billiard rooms evenings, while the rest of the crowd were seeing the sights, and retiring early to our beds. Murray played only occasionally, since he had a bad arm which caused his withdrawal from professional ball. Those who question the value of training for our college teams will find it interesting to note that while this lack of training on the part of the majority seemed to have little effect on their fielding, Cook and I between us made more hits during the trip than were made by the other seven put together. Evidently training does have some effect on one's batting eye.

Near the close of the junior year we received, and with some excitement accepted, an invitation to take part in an intercollegiate baseball tournament which was to be held that summer in connection with the World's Fair at Chicago. The project was a brain-storm of Alonzo Stagg, a recent graduate of Yale, a famous pitcher in his time, and afterwards a more famous football coach in western universities. He had hoped and expected to enroll a large number of the most prominent colleges, and it was because we thought this expectation was going to be realized that we welcomed the chance to join. We had one of our best teams that year, the winner of the " Little Three " championship as it turned out, and we were not reluctant to take our chances in higher circles. On the other hand, the lure of the Fair itself would probably have proved sufficient, even if we had not had the other interest referred to. Great was our disappointment when we reached Chicago to discover that most of the college nines had decided to stay out of the tournament, and that the only ones from the East besides ourselves were those of Wesleyan, the University of Vermont, and the so-called Yale Law School nine. This last aggregation was made up of players from the graduate schools of Yale, the new rule debarring these men from regular college nines having gone into operation that year. The regular Yale varsity nine, which we had met on several occasions on our regular college schedule, was not present.

When we reached Chicago, we found that teams repre-

senting western and southern colleges had already completed their schedule, and that our first game was to be
played against the winner of this group, the University
of Virginia. It was a close game and we won it by a margin
of only two runs, the final score being Amherst 8 and University of Virginia 6. As a result of this defeat, our southern
friends departed. The teams remaining, which were to
fight it out for the championship, were Wesleyan, Vermont, and Yale Law School. The game with Wesleyan was
exceedingly close, Amherst finally winning 7 to 6. That
with Vermont was equally so with a final score of Amherst
1, Vermont 0. Then we faced the tussle with Yale Law
School. It was to be a series of two games out of three. The
first game went to Yale 1 to 0, but the closeness of the
score evidently alarmed Stagg, who had counted on his
own college to carry off the honors. How badly it alarmed
him we did not realize at the moment, but we were shortly
to be enlightened. To our surprise, the next game with
Yale was announced to be played two days later. This
would give Colby, our mainstay in the pitcher's box, and
none too strong physically at best, only one day of rest
between two hard games. Up to that time we had been
allowed at least three days between games, and we protested vigorously but to no avail. Our distress became more
acute when the night before this second game was to be
played, the battery of the regular Yale nine, Carter and
Kedzie, without doubt the best college battery in the
country that year, showed up at our hotel. Carter and I
had already become the best of friends and I asked him,
with some concern, what brought him out there at that
particular time. His reply that Stagg had telegraphed them
to come out to play the next day's game, took my breath

away for, when graduates were debarred from participation on the regular College nine, the team which they collected and called the Law School nine was accepted as just as distinct from the College nine as would be the team from another institution. Again our vigorous protest went for naught, and the game began.

For four innings, Colby stood the strain, but in the fifth, a ligament in his arm gave way. Gregory, our substitute, was called in to the box, but before the inning was over nine runs had been scored by our opponents. Gregory had his opponents well in hand from then on, but of course the damage had been done. We could not hit Carter. The game ended with a 9 to 0 score against us, and the trophy, which was awaiting the winner of the tournament, was officially assigned to Yale.

Fortunately, the World's Fair, and especially the Midway, claimed most of our time and interest, so that we did not grieve too badly over our misfortune on the diamond. We were mad though, and justly so, and we read with no little satisfaction the vigorous protests of the Chicago newspapers over the unfair treatment we had received. No words were spared by the editors in expressing their disgust with the whole affair and extending their sympathy to us. Later, *Outing*, a magazine which in those days carried the articles of Casper Whitney, the then collegiate athletic mentor, whose All-America teams were the only ones so recognized, had his say on the fiasco, and here is the way he put it:

We are very glad to learn that the Yale Law School Nine will no longer be represented among the college teams. It was, from beginning to end, of no particular credit to amateur sport. Its last triumphant exit at Chicago was characteristic of the organization. With the aid of some players from their regular varsity nine, it finally beat Amherst, to become the Intercollegiate Champion for 1893. The handsome trophy that was awarded it has been placed in the Yale trophy room. Of course, it means nothing and everybody so understands.

So ended the Chicago venture. In spite of our disappointment over the outcome of the games themselves, we carried home a lot of happy memories. When not on the field we could always be found on the fair grounds, most often somewhere along the famous Midway, where we tried out every crooked device so glowingly advertised by the fakirs who crowded the gilded sides. In company with our good friends from Wesleyan and the University of Vermont, we haunted the place until the last minute allowed us by Stagg and his fellow-promoters and had a royal good time. While we brought no special credit to Amherst by this jaunt, I am sure that we did the college no harm. At least we won the good will of the fans who attended the games and who, when they learned of our shabby treatment, rallied to our support as vigorously as if they had been Amherst men themselves.

In spite of the general interest that prevailed throughout the college in the nineties, college spirit, as that much abused term is generally defined, was nothing to brag about. Indeed it had reached a low ebb. Both Dartmouth and Williams displayed far more of it than anything Amherst could show, and that fact was a subject of frequent comment. As I visit Amherst from time to time in these recent years, watch the bonfire and listen to firecrackers and speeches at the celebrations — if that is the right word

— on the nights before games, my thoughts go back to the time we unexpectedly won the baseball championship for Amherst in the spring of '93 by beating Dartmouth on her home grounds in two games played on successive days. We had not the remotest idea of accomplishing this feat, but we did the impossible, thanks to the remarkable pitching of Colby and Gregory, and that too against Dartmouth's famous battery of O'Connor and Ranney, which ranked at the very top among the college batteries of their day.

The news of our victory was flashed to Amherst at once; but unfortunately our manager had insisted on arranging games for the two following days at Burlington with the University of Vermont team. None of us had the slightest interest in these latter games, and I myself had protested vigorously when the schedule was being made out. The manager was asking altogether too much. Our pitchers were in no shape for this added ordeal, and we resorted to substitutes, losing both games by good scores. This troubled us little, however, as we were still exulting in the fact that we had won the pennant — so why worry?

On our return to Amherst that Saturday night we looked in vain for some evidence that the college appreciated our feat. Not a soul was at the station to meet us, and we made our way to our rooms, sore and disgusted. When later our mates ventured to express their feelings, about all they had to say was, "What happened to you fellows up in Burlington?" We were too mad to answer, and it was not uncommon to hear a member of the squad say somewhat under his breath, "If we had been playing for Williams, we would have got some credit for this. There's no college spirit in Amherst anyway." Of course, that was not quite true, but it is true that at both Williams and Dartmouth, the latter college especially, so-called college spirit was something very pronounced and noisy. At Dartmouth in fact it took some curious ways of expressing itself. Here is one example.

For a number of years it had been the custom for visiting teams to stay at the Hanover Inn on the edge of the campus. It had also been the custom for the Dartmouth undergraduates to send relays, chosen from their number, to " horn " the visiting team throughout the night, disturbing, if not making impossible, their sleep and so rendering them easier victims for the next day's strife. By chance, some of the Harvard members of the Boston Athletic Association team with which I had played previously, had warned me of this practice of our New Hampshire friends and revealed that they had escaped it by taking quarters at a little inn over across the river in the quiet village of Norwich, Vermont. Acting on their suggestion the Amherst team stayed at this inn on this occasion and were in the pink of condition for the games in consequence.

If our Amherst mates were slow to show their appreciation of these pennant-winning victories, at least our Dartmouth friends were not slow in showing their disappointment. The college band, generously backed by all the noise-making devices known to undergraduates, kept up a constant racket throughout both games, and personal and not generally flattering remarks directed at individual players rolled in a steady stream from excited fans on the sidelines and bleachers. We always felt, and I think with some justice, that the opening play in the first game was our lucky omen and started us on the road to victory. The first Dartmouth batter lifted a high foul which dropped straight towards the center of the band crowded as close as it dared get, and a bit closer than the law allowed, to third base. "Tute" Ellis, our third baseman, figured at once where the ball was destined to drop, but undismayed dashed headlong into the startled musicians, overturning more than one in the process, and emerged with the ball safely in his hands. On that play at the very outset of the game we stole a lot of Dartmouth's courage and added an equal amount to our own.

The second game was played in the morning. It was short and snappy; and it was a happy, yelling group that tumbled into the waiting bus for the ride across the river to Norwich and the noon meal. On the corner of the intersecting streets across from the Hanover Inn, about one hundred disappointed undergraduates were waiting to give us a proper send-off. And they did it with a will. "Amherst, Amherst, God damn Amherst," they chanted over and over in unison. We grinned and returned their taunts in good measure, until the ominous rattle of stones against the sides of the open bus prompted us to slide to the floor as galloping horses, swaying bus, and happy occupants left the historic town of Hanover behind them. While we were devouring our noon meal the president of the Dartmouth Y. M. C. A. appeared to apologize for the behavior of his mates and to assure us that this boisterous group in no sense represented the college or truly expressed the attitude of the student body as a whole. We were in no mood to question the truth of his contentions, for we had enjoyed the experience even more than had our demonstrative friends, and the memory of it was to prove a fine antidote to soreness we justly felt over the indifference of our own college mates.

Only a few years ago Dartmouth and Amherst met in a football game on the former's campus. It was the first time such a contest had been held in many years, and our New Hampshire friends went out of their way to make it a memorable occasion. Among other attractions they arranged a big dinner at which the players, coaches, and prominent student leaders from each college were placed at tables together with their opposite numbers. Several speakers talked on athletics in general, and I was invited to speak for the "old timers." It was an interesting occasion, and as I looked over the crowd, with the Dartmouth representatives exerting themselves to play generous hosts to the Amherst visitors, my thoughts turned back to that day in Hanover years before and the methods then employed to extend hospitality. The strange contrast was accentuated by the fact that the room in which this modern banquet was being held was located only a few yards from the corner which we of those earlier and somewhat rougher days had reason to remember so vividly. The songs which punctuated the program, and which came from the throats of Dartmouth and Amherst men alike, were a bit different to say the least from the hymn of hate which had rung so pleasantly in our ears almost on the same spot some forty odd years before.

The speakers of the Dartmouth group had much to say on this occasion of the early founding of the college and especially of the pious lives and hopes of the founders and those who immediately followed them. Surely the Hanover college was deeply steeped in religious and spiritual traditions. I had never fully realized this before, the earlier contacts having been of a more secular kind. But the new knowledge prompted a thought. Was it just possible, I said

to myself, that we old-timers had misinterpreted that parting slogan flung at us by our disappointed friends as we
took our hasty leave. We had thought it a curse. Perhaps
after all it was intended for a prayer. But curse or prayer,
I am confident that I and the members of my team would
not, even to this day, swap our experience for all the dinners and speakers and all the rest offered in these modern,
more sedate, but distinctly softer times.

From Amherst's standpoint no more heartbreaking game
was ever played on Pratt Field than the commencement
game with Williams in my senior year. Because of the injury to his arm incurred in the final game of the World's
Fair series the year before, Colby had been unable to pitch
this year and Gregory had to carry the load practically
alone. He did a splendid job, but one man could not do it
all, especially with a rather weak-hitting team to back him
up. But in this final game Gregory gave probably the best
exhibition of his career, and it was through no fault of his
that Amherst lost that game and her last chance to win
the league pennant.

For thirteen exciting innings the teams struggled. It
was a pitchers' battle from the start, as the final record
of hits clearly reveals, three hits being Williams's limit and
seven Amherst's. But the final blow, a home run by J.
Lynch of Williams in the final inning, settled matters. Up
to this point each team had secured one run only. That of
Williams was a clean gift, the result of errors by Landis,
who out of nine chances had contributed five glaring errors, most of them wholly inexcusable. Except for these,
Amherst should easily have won a 1 to 0 shutout. I mention these details because of something very unusual

which occurred later, the complete story of which I rate as probably the most dramatic and revealing of any connected with my Amherst associations.

Several days after the Williams game I was alone in my room at the Psi U house, dismantling quarters which with all their happy associations of college days I was to leave for good. It was late at night, a bit after midnight in fact. Most of the other occupants of the house had already left for their homes, and at the moment I was the only person in the building. It was a gloomy and homesick graduate who was suddenly aroused from his dreaminess by a knock on the door. " Come in," I shouted. There was no response. " Come in," I yelled more loudly. The door slowly opened, and in the semi-darkness I recognized the figure of Bobby Landis. " In heaven's name, what brings you here at this time of night, Bob? " I stammered. There was no reply, and I started towards him. Still in the shadows he startled me by a mumbling response in his deep, gruff voice, " I couldn't leave town without speaking to you. You've been the best friend I've had in college, and I've treated you like a skunk. I was drunk the night before the Williams game. It's all over now, but I just had to get this off my chest."

" Well, you're telling me no news," I laughed. " I knew that at the time. Forget it. That's what I mean to do."

Before I had finished the figure disappeared, and I heard Bob hurrying down the stairs. Repeated and urgent requests that he should come back brought no response, and I heard the front door slam behind him. I found the next morning that Bob had left town at an early hour, and I did not see him again until five years later at our first class reunion.

During those intervening five years death had claimed several of the finest members of the class. Landis himself had contracted tuberculosis in the hospital where he was serving as an interne, after having completed his medical course at the Jefferson Medical School in Philadelphia, and had passed a couple of years at Saranac fighting for his life. He had won the fight and seemed his old-time vigorous self when we gathered to celebrate our first reunion.

The committee in charge of the program for our anniversary celebration had decided to bring back so far as possible the settings of the college life we had known in undergraduate days. One item included was a class prayer meeting, a customary function of all classes in the nineties. Several men had been asked to pay brief tributes at this meeting to the members of the class who had died. Because of the outstanding characters of these, the eulogies were justly laudatory. The class turned out as a whole for this meeting, although many of them had rarely if ever attended prayer meetings in undergraduate days. Landis was one of these latter. I sat with him and later strolled down to our headquarters in his company. Try as I would, I could not get a word out of him on this brief trip. He appeared strangely morose. As we turned in to the yard of the house where we were staying, I finally let go. "For heaven's sake, Bobby," I said with some feeling, "what ails you? Have you lost your tongue? You haven't peeped since we left the chapel."

"Do you know what I've been thinking?" he finally grumbled in his low voice. "I couldn't help thinking of the good things that were said about the fellows who have gone. They deserved it all too. You know how close I came to cashing in. Well, I was just wondering if I had passed on what the hell good thing anyone could have thought up to say about me." I laughed outright, but Bob was seriously in earnest.

The reunion over, I did not see Bob again for many years, since my own engagements at Andover made it impossible to get to Amherst at commencement times, except once or twice for the last hours only of the festivities, and on those occasions Bob had left before my arrival or had been unable to join with the group at all. I knew in a hazy way that he had been practicing medicine in Philadelphia, but that was about all.

Some years later when our class was looking forward to its thirty-fifth reunion in 1929, I received a letter from Robert Esty, Amherst '97, then resident in Philadelphia. The contents amused me. In substance this is what Esty had to say. Since you are now a member of the Board of Trustees of Amherst College, you doubtless have something to say about the award of honorary degrees and I would suggest that you consider seriously the claims of Bobby Landis to such an honor. In my judgment no one is more worthy of this award.

I at once wrote Esty that while I deeply appreciated his interest in Landis and while there was no member of our class for whom I had a deeper affection, Bob was about the last man, on the basis of his college record as I recalled it, who could be said to have earned this distinction, and that the trustees were accustomed to base such awards on scholastic and other high achievements and not on personal friendships. Esty's reply was a vigorous one, and in it he gave me to understand that I did not know what I was talking about and that he only asked that I should look up for myself Bobby's record and pass my own judgment on it. He was confident that the record would speak for itself.

My first reaction was to let the matter rest. Second thought led me to feel that in justice to all concerned the record deserved investigation. So I wrote to an old friend, then Dean of the Medical School of the University of Pennsylvania, who had in earlier years been a fellow-teacher of mine at the Hill School, and asked him if there was anything in Esty's suggestion. Dr. Hatfield's reply came promptly and gave me something of a jolt. " There's so much in it," he wrote, " that you will have to give me a little time in which to collect the data you need." A few days later the data arrived; and it took two closely typed sheets of paper to contain them. The list of my old friend"s achievements included several books on tuberculosis, of which Landis was author or co-author, and scores of articles he had published in leading medical magazines. " And this is only part of the story," wrote Hatfield. " As a matter of fact at least two of the books listed are standard textbooks in most of the top medical schools of the country, and there is not a man in the profession, especially those interested in tuberculosis, who does not await eagerly the last word on the subject from Landis's pen." By the time I had recovered from my surprise, Dr. Hatfield's letter and accompanying information were in the hands of the Honorary Degrees Committee of the trustees. A unanimous vote to the effect that Landis be granted the honorary degree of Doctor of Science at the coming commencement was promptly recorded, and later confirmed by the full board.

Almost all of the living members of the class of Ninety-Four had returned for the reunion, and all of these were on hand to lead the applause when their classmate received his diploma and hood on the commencement stage, though many, who remembered Landis only as an undergraduate, were still clearly puzzled to know what it was all about.

At our reunion headquarters Landis and I had rooms on the top floor and on opposite sides of the hallway. It was late at night when we headed for our beds after the excitement of that eventful day. Somewhere around two or three o'clock in the morning I was awakened by a noise and light across the hall. It was a hot night and doors throughout the house had been left open. The light in Bobby's room attracted my attention and I decided to investigate. To my surprise I discovered the occupant, still fully dressed, leaning against the bureau and seemingly toying with articles resting on its top.

"Why in the deuce haven't you gone to bed?" I said as I approached.

There was no reply and I pursued my inquiry. Finally he looked up in a sort of a dazed way and said, "What's the use of going to bed. I can't sleep." Before I could answer he went on in his customary gruff tone, "Amherst has given me a degree. I don't deserve it. It's a joke. What in hell did I ever do in Amherst to earn it, except loaf and make a mess of things."

"Look here, Bob," I broke in, "Amherst isn't giving you this degree for anything you did or did not do in college days, but as a just reward for what you have done since. You had to start from behind scratch too, and you've gone so fast and so far that the rest of us haven't been able to keep up with you or even see you for the dust you've left behind. If anyone deserves a degree from Amherst, you do. And let me tell you, I've always counted you one of my best friends, and today I'm as proud as a peacock to count you such; prouder than I ever was in my life."

He lifted his head slowly and looked at me out of his dark eyes, which were just showing signs of tears. Then throwing his arms over the top of the bureau he buried his face in them and burst into uncontrollable sobs. It was some time before I could quiet him and almost lift his limp form onto the bed. When he seemed finally to have quieted down, I went back to my bed and eventually fell asleep.

I rose early that morning and at once made my way to Bob's room. But Bob had left still earlier, and no one, as I found out later, had seen or heard him go. A week or two later I received from him a scribbled penciled note which read:

Dear Al:
      A great peace has come over me.
                      Yours,
                            Bob

From that day on, I made it a point whenever I found myself in Philadelphia to look Landis up at his home in Haverford. A recurrence of the tuberculosis from which he had suffered in those earlier days had him once more in its grip, centering its attack on his throat. He fought it with his former courage, though he knew that it was only a question of time before it would win the final round. For the last two or three years he could speak only in whispers, but he still met some of his appointments at the Phipps Institute as a lecturer and continued a limited practice among his private patients, especially among the Negroes of the poorer section of the city. I had learned only late in his life of the task he had set himself of helping the colored population of Philadelphia, more than half of whom were unable to pay him anything for his services.

"How did you happen to take that job on yourself?" I once asked him.

His whispered reply was characteristic. "You see, Al," he said, "nobody else was looking after them and the poor devils were shot full of tuberculosis. Someone had to do the job. Anyway," he added, "they gave me a wonderful chance to study at close range the disease in all its manifestations and I learned a lot."

If the Williams game at Amherst in 1894 was a heart-breaker, the final one at Williamstown the following Saturday was so unusual as to deserve a more special designation than I can give it. Its setting can only be described as a comedy of errors. Its finish was dramatic.

The custom in those days was for Amherst and Williams to schedule their last two games during the commencement season so that returning alumni and guests could see their own nines in action. Unless games were to be played on consecutive days, which would be difficult at best, it was agreed that in alternate years each college should have the privilege of holding a game on its home grounds during the days of the actual commencement festivities. In 1894 this privilege fell to Williams, and Amherst was due to cross bats with her ancient rival on Saturday of commencement week. Arrangements had long been completed and the customary special train to carry the players back had been promised. On Friday morning, to our consternation, word came from the railroad authorities in Springfield that owing to unexpected developments the special would have to be canceled. Schmuck, our manager, hurried to Springfield in a last and vain attempt to persuade the railroad to reconsider its decision. He returned late in the evening, crestfallen and thoroughly mad. The railroad would not budge and the train was out.

The problem which confronted us so unexpectedly was a tough one. Three of the four seniors on the team and one junior were members of the Cotillion Club, which was to hold its big dance of the season that Saturday night. The young ladies we had invited for commencement were due to arrive Saturday morning. Without this special train we would have little chance to get back to Amherst before Sunday morning, as the last regular train out of Williamstown left the Berkshires just a bit too early to enable the players to make it after a game of ordinary length. What could we do? Our commencement guests could not be left to shift for themselves at that late hour. And the cotillion was the one event, even more so than the senior prom to follow, which many of us counted the high spot on the commencement program. We wrestled earnestly till late at night with our baffling problem and finally concluded that since Amherst was already out of the race, it would make little difference to us who won this final game and that hence we would be justified in sending substitutes to fill our places. Swift action followed, and we pulled several sleepy freshmen out of their beds and finally made it clear that this was no dream, but that they were to represent the college as members of the varsity nine at Williamstown next day. With the aid of one of our regular substitutes they would just round out a full nine. Smith, the only senior not interested in the dance, lived in Westfield and was to meet the group in Northampton Saturday morning.

The news that he was to captain the strange aggregation was to be conveyed to him when he appeared.

So far so good. But it was a disgruntled and surly lot that we had to deal with at the railroad station next morning. The freshmen were not sorry to have this unusual chance, but the regular members were naturally sore.

The train had pulled in and the members of the team were climbing aboard, when I turned to Pete Fay, the driver of Paige's station coach, and said casually, "You've put the bat bag on, I suppose." Pete had always had the job of stopping at the grandstand on Pratt Field when teams were to leave town to gather up and bring to the station not only the bat bag but gloves, balls, catcher's mask and protector as well.

"God, I clean forgot them," Pete stammered as some of the ruddy color left his face.

"You'll have to borrow from Williams," we yelled to the disconcerted group on the rear platform as the train pulled away. Rather sheepishly we made our way back to our rooms to await the arrival of our guests.

Smith met the team in Northampton as expected, but the news of his new assignment and the evidence of our duplicity left him, according to reports, the maddest man in the county. At Greenfield there was a half-hour's wait for the connecting train, and several members hustled up the street in search of bats and balls. They returned with two bats, for one of which they paid a half dollar and the other a quarter. This was the extent of their equipment when they disembarked from the train at Williamstown, though fortunately each man carried his own uniform. Even our scorer had been provided with one, for we had tardily discovered the night before that the crew we had so hastily

collected totaled only nine men and the rules required
that each team must have ten men in uniform to meet possible emergencies. Howard Noyes was a good scorer, but
nature had certainly not designed him for an athlete. In
addition he was terribly near sighted and wore probably
the thickest glasses ever seen on the college campus. I
doubt whether he could have distinguished a baseball
from a football if either had come his way. But he was duly
garbed, and in evident embarrassment took his seat on the
bench. The requirements of the rules had been met anyway.

When this strange Amherst team appeared on Weston
Field, Smith faced a really tough situation. Williams was
so sure they would win that an enthusiastic manager had
even sent out to the alumni postcards carrying a picture
of the Williams nine and in big letters an invitation to
come back and see Williams's first " Championship Team "
in several years. The alumni had responded generously,
and the crowd on Weston Field that afternoon was the
largest on record up to that time. But the lack of familiar
faces among the Amherst contingent was speedily noted
by the Williams players, and Amherst's new captain was
bombed with searching questions. He replied as best he
could, but the Berkshire lads grew only the madder. Something had been put over on them. They had been insulted
indeed, and they did not hesitate to express their feelings
in the strongest language at their command. And when
Smith ventured somewhat timidly the request that balls,
bats, and gloves be loaned from the Williams store, the
storm really broke. Eventually the request was grudgingly
granted, and a bit later the game itself began.

In the meantime Smith had had a bright thought. Why

not shorten the game and thus win the chance of catching the regular afternoon train out of Williamstown and avoid the necessity of passing the night away from home? Approaching the captain and manager of his opponents he made the suggestion. A storm of abuse was the answer he encountered. Amherst had duped them. Amherst had insulted them and the big crowd on the field as well. And Amherst would take the consequences willy-nilly. Visions of victory with the winner's score running into double figures were not to go unrealized through unmerited generosity. And the game was on.

Williams had good reason to expect a victory. Her battery, Lewis, pitcher, who later played with the Boston Red Sox, and Draper, catcher, was one of the best that any of the three colleges then comprising the league had ever produced; and the rest of the team were well above the average. But she had not counted on the possibility of Gregory, Amherst's twirler, repeating his outstanding performance of the earlier game at Amherst, especially with a mixed and largely unknown team at his back. From the start the game proved close and exciting, a pitchers' battle. At the end of the seventh inning Williams led 2 to 1. Had the game ended then as Smith had proposed, both game and pennant would have gone to Williams. But the last two innings completely changed the picture. Gregory was at his best, while his team-mates played as if inspired. They landed on Lewis for a goodly number of hard, clean hits, including several for extra bases, and when the ninth inning closed had captured the game 5 to 2. Smith glanced at his watch. " Come on, boys," he shouted. " Grab your things and head for the train." They piled into the waiting hacks and reached the station just as the train was pulling in. Dressing in the baggage car, cheering, singing, and banging each other around in uncontrolled glee, they arrived late that night in Amherst.

During the course of the cotillion dance rumors had reached us that Amherst had won. We grinned at each other and put it all down as an attempt of some wag to jolly us. Not for a moment could we make ourselves believe that such an impossibility had actually occurred. It was not till the middle of the next morning that the truth was rudely brought home. Accompanied by my commencement partner, I was just entering the walk that led from behind Johnson Chapel through the grove to the church, when a window in South College opened with a bang and a voice sharp and disconcerting rang out, " You big stiff! Oh, you has-been! Now we know what's been the matter with your old team. Too bad we didn't find it out sooner." And when the baccalaureate service was over and we could get hold of a morning paper, the story faced us in print. The few hours that remained of our college course were made anything but comfortable for us by our justly exulting friends.

That we had no professional coaches in my college days is something for which I have always been grateful. On the field we were not automatons, pulled here and there by strings from the players' bench and with our eyes constantly roving in that direction, lest we miss some signal from the professional boss and perhaps in consequence suffer public humiliation at the hands of this hired autocrat — something I have often witnessed on college playing fields in this streamlined age. Our teams may have lacked a bit in the way of finesse, but at least what we did or did not do was our own. The authority of the captain was complete and final. He selected his team, planned strategy, and directed actual play, but he was never an autocrat, and every member of his team contributed his full and valuable share of criticism and advice. This responsibility, which we took so seriously and which has now been so largely lost, was one of the greatest, if not indeed the greatest, of values derived from athletic sports and competitive games. I honestly pity those who are deprived of it today.

But if we did not have coaches, we did have helpers who voluntarily contributed to the success of our teams. One of these was George Cadwell, officially the caretaker of the grounds on Pratt Field, a real baseball fan and as keenly interested in our success as was any member of the team itself. The baseball nines I was privileged to captain during my junior and senior years owed a lot to this unheralded and enthusiastic friend and were always glad to acknowledge the debt. One of our most difficult problems was to find competent men who could bat flies to the outfielders in practice. Under ordinary conditions these had to be recruited from substitutes or pitchers, and neither proved satisfactory. George was the ideal man for the job and he took it on with zest. The grounds may have suffered, but the nine did not, and George from the start refused to content himself with knocking easily caught flies, but insisted that the fielders should stretch themselves to the limit and learn from practice that they could reach balls that before had seemed impossible to retrieve. And the discovery made them all the more eager to better their performance, so that George was constantly urged to " hit them farther away." Hour after hour and day after day this tireless helper kept at his task until the work of our outfielders became famous.

A striking illustration of the value of Cadwell's work was revealed in the opening game with Williams on Pratt Field in the spring of 1894 by a spectacular play contributed by Cheney, our center fielder. A Williams batter drove a liner well over the center fielder's head, which bore all the earmarks of a home run. With the click of the bat Cheney turned, and without once looking at the flying ball, raced for the open field beyond. At precisely the exact second he turned his head while still at full speed, leaped into the air, and with his gloved hand pulled down the flying sphere. I doubt whether Pratt Field has ever recorded a more brilliant play. As he made his way to the bench at the end of the inning amid the plaudits of the crowd and his fellow-players Cheney turned to Cadwell and grunted, " I owe that to you, George." It was a nice and well reserved tribute, and to this day George delights to recount the incident.

Others among our town friends did their bit as opportunities offered. The football squad was always lacking enough spare men to make up a second eleven, and local players from the high school and elsewhere frequently, and with little urging, filled in the gaps. This proved helpful to the Amherst team and supplied the youngsters themselves with valuable experience. I think this practice must have been intensified after I left college, for a few years later I crossed its trail in an unexpected and amusing way.

My predecessor at Andover, Principal Bancroft, had become disturbed over increasing rumors that our friends and rivals at Exeter were indulging in the then somewhat common practice of including " ringers " in their athletic squads. He was especially concerned over a fellow named Donovan, who had gained fame as a catcher on the Northampton nine, and knowing of my earlier contacts with that outfit, asked me to make a quiet investigation of Donovan's amateur status. Through Northampton friends and others I made inquiries, the results of which certainly did not strengthen Donovan's standing as an amateur. But the investigation uncovered something else that was wholly unsuspected, namely that three of Amherst's Negro citizens had played that previous fall on the Exeter football eleven. Smith, Bias, and Till were the culprits. Bias was a local teamster, Till turned the crank of Deuel's ice-cream freezer, and Smith, so far as I knew, could claim no steady occupation. I assumed that they had learned their football on Pratt Field, for I doubt whether any of them had reached even high school status in their home town. Anyway they played in the Exeter-Andover game that fall, in a contest sparkling with fights and almost resulting in bloodshed, which led the school authorities to call off for the immediate future any further games between these famous academies. A few days after the game in question the three "ringers" were back on their Amherst jobs. Whether they had even registered as members of the institution whose colors they upheld so vigorously that day I was never able to discover. There was a bit of irony in the situation, for Smith was the son of my own mother's cook and butler and had passed a good bit of his youthful days in and near our home kitchen. My Andover friends never tired of twitting me about this.

When I came to Amherst, my mother had made it clear, and I had accepted her decision, that football was not to be included in my athletic activities. She had two objections to offer. First, she felt that tennis and baseball together would take all the time I could properly spare from my studies. Second, from my brother's experience with broken bones she was sure that it would be much safer for me if I left the game severely alone.

Late in the fall of my sophomore year I was given the surprise of my life when the manager of the football team appeared at my room one night and announced that my mother had given her consent to my playing in the three last championship games. Stevens Institute, for some reason, was at that time a member of the league. Dartmouth, Williams, and Amherst were the other three members. The game with Dartmouth, which was to be played at Hanover, was scheduled for the following Saturday. The news came to me Wednesday night and I would not accept it as true until I had seen my mother in person the next morning and had the truth confirmed from her own lips. I found her terribly upset, actually in tears, to think that she had yielded, but when I discovered that she had been attacked by the manager and captain of the team and Old Doc himself, who had been induced by these two missionaries to join them in the assault, I understood why. Anyway, the deed was done, and I was scheduled to play at Hanover on Saturday.

Except for the fact that I had played tennis again that fall, my partner in the finals being Reid, later to become the famous dean of the American Cathedral in Paris, and had always kept in pretty good physical condition, I was wholly unfit to engage on that short notice in as strenuous a game as the contest at Dartmouth always proved to be. I had not had on a football suit or been in a scrimmage that fall. Furthermore, there was to be no scrimmage on that Thursday, and Friday was to be spent in travel. Consequently, all I could do was to go down to the field, don a suit, run around the track to strengthen my wind, and learn as many signals as I could. On the trip to Hanover the next day, at various station stops the squad piled out and went through signals again, so that by the time we appeared on the field, I had a fairly good knowledge of the signals, especially those that concerned me intimately, and had a little better wind than before, but physically I was about as soft as a wet dish-rag. The captain assured me that since my specialty was kicking and my condition naturally below par, Amherst would play a kicking game from the start, hoping in that way to gain an advantage that would carry through the rest of the game, and that he would then take me out. As a matter of fact this program was early discarded, the game ended in a tie, 14 to 14, and I played through to the end.

It should be remembered that in those days substitutes were not permitted except for good. If a man was forced to leave the field, he stayed on the bench, and the one who took his place stayed in the game. Further, there were no quarter periods with their brief intermissions to give the players a chance to catch their breath; and the halves were of three-quarters of an hour each in length. Add to all this the fact that the game was played on the old Hanover common with its numerous gravel cross-walks and that football suits were much less padded than they are today, and it can be easily realized that the contest was no tea-party, especially for me. I only know that on the trip down on the sleeper that night I was ready to pay anyone to shoot me to relieve me of the physical agony I suffered. It seemed as if everything inside of me had been torn to pieces; and on my return to Amherst I was compelled for the next three days to limp about on crutches.

My roommate, Herm Cheney, knowing that I was physically unfit for this strenuous experience and fearing disaster had, unknown to me at the time, taken a later train to Hanover and watched the struggle from the sidelines. On the trip home that night he played the part of a voluntary nurse, rubbing my aching muscles and bones unflinchingly from White River Junction to Northampton.

"Don't be afraid of Dartmouth," snapped Old Doc in staccato tones at the chapel "pep" meeting on the morning of our departure for Hanover. "Don't be afraid of Dartmouth. Dartmouth is famous for only two things, Daniel Webster and some big elm trees."

Webster's ghost may have been lurking in the background during the game, but I am confident that it was one of those big elm trees that my nose encountered when I made my first attempt to buck the Dartmouth line. With Lewis and Haskell at center and guard, both of whom were to play on the Harvard eleven later and the former to become an All-America center, our quarterback had figured that gains could be rightly counted on at that spot. But instead of the expected hole I smashed into these two stalwarts reeling back under the impetus of their two more stalwart opponents, and with disastrous results. When I recovered from the shock someone else had the ball and I a broken and bloody nose, the condition of which was certainly not improved as the game progressed.

The game with Stevens Institute the following Saturday proved to be an easy victory for Amherst, but that with Williams a week later turned out as unfortunately as the game at Hanover two weeks before, since neither side was able to score. The Williams game too was played in about the deepest mud of which Pratt Field at its worst could boast.

As a result of these tie games, no one of the colleges involved could claim the championship that year and no pennant was awarded. If these strenuous games resulted in no championship, they did produce results of totally different kinds, some of them not to be recorded until many years later.

In the Dartmouth game, Amherst made the last touchdown shortly before time was called and directly between the goal posts. This was important in those years for, under the rules, goals had to be kicked from a point directly opposite the spot where the touchdown was made. As a rule those made close to the goal posts resulted in easy goals for the scoring team. When they had to be attempted from the side of the field, it was a different story, especially if the wind was blowing.

With the score 14 to 14 and a goal to be kicked from directly in front of the posts, we had justified visions of not only a victory but of a football championship as well, of such significance was that one remaining point.

George Pratt, our goal kicker, duly prepared to meet the test. It was clearly evident, however, that he was nervous, for he could not seem to satisfy himself that the ball was being properly held for him and on at least two occasions, as he was about to kick, decided to make readjustments. When at last he booted the ball, it bobbed along on the top of the ground instead of sailing over the crossbar as he had anticipated, and the chances for victory and pennant alike disappeared. Pratt never got over this, and without saying a word to anybody of his intention, carried home a football with him that next spring and practised daily at kicking goals, with the result that in the Williams game at Williamstown the following fall, a game played on a muddy field with sleet and snow beating down on the players through it all, a game which Amherst won by the overwhelming score of 60 to 0, Pratt kicked every one of the goals without a mishap and some of them from seemingly impossible angles.

The other results involved were those which affected me. Early in this Dartmouth game my nose, an all too prominent part of my anatomy for football, had been badly broken. As a result, the nasal passages were practically closed and after suffering from it for several years, I decided that a plumbing job was in order. On the recommendation of Old Doc I put myself in the hands of Dr. Leland in Boston, an Amherst graduate and a leading nose specialist of his time. By the time he had finished with me he had gathered in a little over $400, which represented about all of my savings from three years of teaching. Dr. Leland at that time was supporting the gymnasium prize as it was called, a prize given annually to the class which excelled at an exhibition of marching and dumbbell exercises. I never ceased to banter Old Doc about this, and accused him of overpersuading my mother to let me play football that fall, placing me in Dr. Leland's hands, and all for the purpose of sustaining the Leland gym prize.

Some years later still, Dartmouth was gracious enough to present me with an honorary degree at a Commencement Luncheon where the recipients of such degrees were required to make their appreciative addresses. I reminded the group of that game at Hanover years before, and thanked the college for its generous, if somewhat delayed, recognition of their obligation to one who had so suffered at the hands of its representatives.

It was many years later still before I faced the final results of that strenuous afternoon's activity. Without previous warning, I had decided to faint away at a faculty meeting one afternoon, and found myself a few hours later in a room at the Phillips House in Boston, awaiting observation. The results of the observation brought me to the surgeon's table and resulted in the extraction of a kidney. Several days later, when I was in condition to discuss the matter with him, the operating surgeon remarked that he would give a good deal to know just what had happened to that battered kidney of mine.

" Just what do you mean by that," I asked.

" Well," he answered, " it was several times its normal size and it was covered with bunches of growths resulting evidently from injuries received a long time ago. You must have had a terrible thumping around that part of your anatomy a good many years ago, probably in your school or college days."

Grinning I replied, " If that's the case, I can give you the day, the hour, and the place." I then related the story of the Dartmouth game of 1891.

" Don't tell me any more," he laughed. " That's enough to account for all this and more, and I'm relieved."

If Dartmouth was generous enough to give me a degree for a broken nose, it evidently never found one suitable for a shattered kidney.

VIII · *Social Life*

SOCIAL ACTIVITIES IN THE early nineties were necessarily restricted. Young ladies, barring the limited number residing in the town itself, were not easily available; and lacking proper representation of the fairer sex, no social function could by any stretch of the imagination be considered a success. Smith and Mount Holyoke colleges, on which Amherst has drawn so heavily in recent years, were still some distance away when horse and buggy and the limited train service to and from Northampton supplied the only means of conveyance. Both, too, led a somewhat cloistered life with exacting regulations to govern the occasional visitors who were bold enough to enter the sacred precincts. This was especially true of Mount Holyoke, where even a student caller must produce evidence of relationship to the young lady on whom he was allowed to call. In my four years at Amherst the girls from this convent-like institution played little if any part in the social life of the college on the hill.

The women of the faculty occasionally invited us to what were called parties at their homes, but these were pretty stiff and wooden affairs and excited little interest. We knew in advance what girls we would meet, and all had their numbers and rating. Dancing at such sedate affairs would have been considered little less than scandalous, and it was so regarded until Mrs. David Todd joined the faculty circle and set tongues wagging and tempers rising by her modern ways and by offering a wholesome if advanced type of entertainment to the socially starved of the students. Several of the older fraternities indulged once or twice a year in rather select dances, really afternoon teas at which dancing was a part of the program, and at which a limited number of girls from Smith were present. Smith in turn held its annual and historic Washington's Birthday " Party," which beggars description. Large numbers of the students attended this and for varying reasons, chiefly, I suppose, because it offered one of the rare chances in the college year to meet and actually talk with the young ladies who were students there. A special train regularly brought them home and at an early hour.

This high spot in the social life of the sister college deserves a paragraph of its own. Among Amherst men it was commonly dubbed " The Starvation Stand-up," " Ten Mile Walk Around," and other equally descriptive and appropriate titles. It was held in the evening and in the largest hall on the college grounds. The crowd that milled around in it was more suggestive of one trapped, when evening trains to the suburbs have been delayed, in the Grand Central Station in New York than of one supposedly attending a " party." Round dancing was strictly forbidden, but square dances were allowed if and when a large enough open space could be found — which was almost never. Refreshments were scanty in the extreme, if indeed the tables from which they were served could ever be located. By the time this gruesome affair was over those who had literally fought their way around were as exhausted as if they had participated in an Amherst-Williams football game. Lest I may seem to exaggerate let me quote from the columns of the *Amherst Student* of those days:

A reception at Smith College is a cross between a funeral and a kettle drum. We should call it a fancy dress ball, but the lights are extinguished at 10 o'clock. We should call it a walking match, but it lacks the element of betting to make it exciting. We should call it a church sociable, but church sociables usually furnish something to gratify the inner man, if it be nothing but ham sandwiches and Sunday School lemonade. We should call it the annual exhibition of the inmates of an orphan asylum, but the contribution box is not circulated. Thus in many respects it differs from the popular amusements of the age. It is, in fact, an anomaly.

And again:

With poetic vision I look forward to a happy millennium when the good old Connecticut Valley will be shocked by two steps of progress — non-compulsory church at Amherst and round dancing at the regular Smith reception.

Verily time has wrought its changes.

Since we lacked outlets for our social ambitions, it was only natural that some of the most daring among us should look beyond the limits which bounded these accepted social functions and seek for something more exciting, if less approved. A welcome outlet for a very few who were fortunate enough to command invitations, was the annual assembly at the City Hall in Springfield the night before the Yale-Harvard football game, which was then regularly held in that city. Others were forced to content themselves with entertainment of lesser grade. The " Company K " balls, staged every little while by the local militia, proved a lure to not a few, and not always with the happiest results. The experience of two of our colleagues who went somewhat farther afield in the search for excitement gave the college a good laugh for many days thereafter.

Most of the fraternity houses had Negro janitors, and every now and then the occupants were adroitly approached and asked to help a worthy cause by purchasing a ticket or two. Neither seller or buyer expected that such tickets would ever be used. So far as I know they never had been before this particular night, when two venture-some lads decided that it would be a lot of fun to attend just to see what the thing was like. They were careful not to mention their plan to any of their friends and agreed that the affair must be kept strictly secret. In due season they appeared at the hall where the dance was in progress, presented their tickets, and were admitted and shown to seats. Here they sat quietly for some time, interested and amused, but strictly minding their own business. At length they noticed that increasing and not too friendly glances were being turned in their direction. A bit later the danc-ing appeared to be slackening and a number of the dancers with several of the ushers went into a huddle in a corner of the room. While the visitors were wondering what it was all about, an usher disentangled himself from the crowd and came timidly towards them.

"I beg yo' pardon," he began, "but I've got to ask yo' to leave de hall."

"But why?" inquired one of the surprised couple. "We haven't done anything. We haven't made any disturbance. And, besides, we paid for the tickets and are entitled to be here."

"Dat's all true," admitted the usher much embarrassed. "Yo've behaved like perfect gent'men and I'm sorry to hef to ask yo' to go."

"But just why then do you ask us to go?" repeated the victim, "I can't understand it."

"Well, yo' see," replied the usher now almost in a panic, "some of de ladies object to de odor."

Our venturesome friends never heard the last of that, when the story leaked out later, and for many weeks their lives were made more than miserable by the gleeful innuendoes of their mates.

If Amherst students were bored by the Smith College "Walk Around," an increasing number of the Smith students themselves were disgusted with it. Unless they counted on the chance to meet some very special "friend," they stayed away. Between the indignant representatives of both institutions numerous "bull sessions," when rare opportunities offered, were held with this "anomaly" the main topic of discussion. All were agreed that it ought to go, but none could say just how. Finally a bright idea was advanced. Since undergraduates were helpless to rid themselves of the thing, why not start something really worth while to offset it? Various suggestions were promptly forthcoming, and one that appealed to all was enthusiastically accepted. Dances in the form of germans were increasing in popularity, and a german was our remedy. We would hire the Capen School gymnasium, just outside the college grounds, and there dance to our hearts' content. But an evening affair had to be ruled out. The dance would cause an uproar among the conservatives anyway, and we did not dare risk increasing that tumult by running a rival show in competition with the staid and historic function sanctioned by the authorities. Besides, an evening affair would have to stop by ten o'clock and that would not give us half the time we needed.

There were five Smith girls and about the same number of Amherst fellows involved in the plot, and for several weeks we worked over our plans. They shaped up eventually as follows. The Capen gym would be secured. The dance would start at ten o'clock in the morning, refreshments would be served at noon, and dancing continue till the middle or late afternoon. And since the evening was denied us, we would do our best to offset that loss by pretending that it was an evening affair. Shades were to be drawn, lights turned on full blast, and those who participated would come in full evening dress. With all arrangements completed, we waited eagerly for the day and the great event. The Father of his Country would have been duly flattered if he could have realized the eagerness with which about a dozen undergraduate promoters in those two famous colleges of the Connecticut Valley anticipated the coming of his birthday that year.

At last the day arrived, heralded in advance by a good old-fashioned New England blizzard, which began its operations the afternoon before. As the storm increased in violence, we decided that it would be prudent to make an early start for our destination, and we headed for Hamp that night. As we disembarked from the train in that famous town, snow whipped by a strong wind was falling thick and fast and piling up in menacing drifts. The one good hotel was about a half mile away, and as we had made no advance reservations we feared that if we reached it we might well find it filled with guests of the college and be turned away with the prospects of plowing around the town through the deepening snow in search of rooms. Just back of the station was a small hotel, so called, which we vaguely understood had none too good a reputation. But it was near at hand and we decided to take a chance. Yes, the clerk assured us, we could be taken care of. He turned the hotel register toward us and held out a pen. The first man to register showed signs of panic, a panic that spread as we in turn glanced at the page before us. The last names entered read " Mr. & Mrs. Blank," and the residence given was " Africa." But we had to go through with it, and after the whole group had been sworn to secrecy we added our names in turn.

The rooms proved fairly good, the breakfast next morning not so bad, and in due time, adorned in our evening clothes, we struggled up the hill over partly plowed roads to the Capen gym. Here the brightly lighted hall with its gay and colorful trimmings speedily restored our spirits. But some of the girls at least were plainly distressed, for word had been received from the railroad officials that trains which were carrying their partners from Williamstown, Hanover, and New Haven would probably not be able to get through, or at best would arrive at a late hour. We from Amherst chuckled over this news, for here was our chance. We had always resented the fact that the tally-hos which brought our fair friends over to the games in Amherst carried altogether too much of our rival's colors. There would be no rivals to bother us today, at least not at the start, and our Smith friends would have to take us on willy-nilly. And in a german that meant that we could count on dancing every number, while wall flowers would be confined to the other sex alone. As germans are no longer the fashion, and modern youth probably does not even know how they were conducted, it is not likely that any of these later-day dance lovers could ever be made to understand the nature of the thrills we got that day in the old Capen gym, when we watched not one but several of Smith's fairest literally racing across the floor in their efforts to be first to reach their chosen partners and deposit their favors in waiting hands. And when it came our turn,

we could coolly stand, casually look over prospective partners, and pick almost at random. Needless to say, our
gloatings were fully matched by the embarrassment pictured on the faces of the waiting girls and the manifest
chagrin of those who were passed by.

When it was all over, even the young ladies admitted
that the affair had been an outstanding success. Before the
end a few fellows from some of the other colleges had
straggled in, but not in sufficient numbers to alter the general picture. Amherst had had her day, and she made the
most of it. The stiff-necked conservatives of Northampton
and especially those of that hue who were connected
with Smith, from then on had not their day but their days
when tongues wagged incessantly and imprecations were
hurled at the perpetrators of this " scandalous outrage."

As I look back over the years, I find no little amusement
in noting the later careers of those then too modern " flap-
pers," who so ably conspired with us to break the old con-
ventions, have a royal good time, and bring down upon
their heads the reproof of their elders. Well, on the whole
they have made a pretty fair record. One, who remained a
spinster through her life, devoted her time, her strength,
and her money to bringing up and educating a number of
nephews and nieces, filling her spare hours with other and
equally commendable charitable activities. Another had
the temerity to return later to her old college as a teacher
and to become eventually the head of her department. A
third was graduated at the head of her class from the Johns
Hopkins Medical School — the first one of her sex to secure
this coveted diploma — and later was appointed superin-
tendent of the Babies Hospital in New York, a position she
held until she married the head of the physics department

in the University of Wisconsin. Another became the principal of one of Boston's best schools for girls, where she did a splendid job as an administrator, an upholder of the highest standards of scholarship, and a wise guide and counselor of the hundreds of girls who were fortunate enough to come under her care. I had the privilege of serving for some years as one of her trustees, until at the time of her retirement several years ago I terminated the connection. The only one of this group, which in college days had so worried their elders, who refused to be sobered by the discipline and exactions of the world outside the college gates was the one who later became my wife.

The truly high spots in our restricted social activities were, of course, the Junior and Senior Promenades. The Cotillion Club, organized in the fall of 1893, was a long step in advance with its fall, winter, and commencement germans, but the privileges it offered were limited to the small and carefully picked group who comprised its membership. The proms, on the other hand, were open to all who wished to attend and were ready to pay the price. As a rule about one half of the class chiefly involved turned out on these occasions, the other three classes supplying smaller quotas. Invited girls came from neighboring cities and often from long distances, especially for the senior affair, when commencement activities were in full swing and members of the graduating class desired to have only their choicest friends on hand. Even so, we had to rely chiefly on Smith, and about one half of the girls present came from the college across the river. But here was the rub. Under the rules of that still conservative institution its students were required to leave the dance promptly on the stroke of midnight. That gave them just time for refreshments and possibly one short dance after. Then they withdrew with their numerous chaperones, and when the commotion of their departure had subsided the gym floor was a sorry sight. A good half of the men present were without partners and could only mill around dejectedly until here and there some of the few girls left happened to have places on their dance cards. " Cutting in " had not then arrived to make dances free fights, and if, as occasionally happened, some lonesome and daring youth assayed the attempt, that attempt was his last. The wind-up of these proms was in consequence a depressing anticlimax.

In my junior year it fell to my lot to be chosen chairman of the class Prom Committee. Having picked with care my four assistants, I called them together to consider possible solutions to the baffling problem presented by the early departure of our Smith College friends. We decided that we needed their help first of all, and negotiations were promptly begun with the members of the " Big Five," as they called themselves, who had so successfully co-operated with us in carrying out the Capen Gym affair. It was their suggestion that we should approach the faculty committee which controlled all social activities at Smith and which had long been known as the " Squelch Committee." And they further insisted, and to my consternation, that I should be the one to make this hazardous contact. They argued that because of my long connections with the town and neighborhood and the fact that my mother conducted a girls' school of her own, I would be the most likely one to obtain a respectful hearing. The other members of my committee were only too glad to shirk the unpleasant task

and eagerly supported the proposal. So in spite of my protests I found myself saddled with a job that filled me with
terror as I contemplated its real meaning.

The Smith "Squelch Committee" was composed of
three members, all spinsters, and none of them young. The
chairman, or chairwoman, was known among her students
as "The Iceberg," and that did not add to my confidence.
Miss Mary Jordan, a brilliant teacher, practically dean of
the college and President Seelye's right bower, was another member. The third I do not recall. My Smith friends
coached me carefully in advance, explaining the peculiarities of each and the best methods of approach. In due season, and in answer to my very polite note requesting an
interview, "The Iceberg" wrote me that she would be
glad to see me and suggested a date for the meeting. "So
I'm to deal only with 'The Iceberg,'" I said to myself, and
the thought and name combined sent the shivers down my
spine. It was a badly scared junior who timidly rang the
bell at Miss Gorham's apartment a few nights later and
was ushered into a sparsely furnished and definitely chilly
room.

I took a hurried glance at "The Iceberg" as she entered
the room and held out her hand to greet me, and the first
impression was not exactly reassuring. With her whitening
hair and immobile face, she offered little hope that my
petition would receive favorable consideration. But with
the first shock behind me, I gathered courage if not eloquence as I presented my case. I pictured as vividly as I
could that forlorn group of Amherst undergraduates who
had spent their hard-earned savings on prom tickets, only
to have their fun snatched from them in the very midst of
the festivities. I embellished this, too, with a bit of added,

if somewhat exaggerated, color, depicting the chagrin of the Smith guests as they were forced to leave their partners in the lurch. Miss Gorham listened patiently, but with no flicker of interest on her changeless face. With the exhaustion of words and breath I finally paused.

"But you see, Mr. Stearns," — the chairman of the Squelch Committee was actually speaking — "we can't permit the young ladies to stay longer for there would be no way to get them back to Northampton at a later hour, and even if there were, we should be wholly unwilling to have them return in the early morning hours."

"Yes," I ventured, "I know that you feel that way, but why do they have to return? Why could they not pass the night in Amherst, provided, of course, proper provision were made for them?"

"And what provision would you suggest?" came the prompt reply.

I had done some rather hazy thinking along this line in preparation for the interview, though without any assurance that any of the plans that had suggested themselves could be carried out, and was a bit appalled at my own nerve when I answered, "Well, we might set aside a dormitory, turn the boys out, and place it entirely at the disposal of the girls and their chaperones. Or we might hire the Amherst House and treat it in the same way. And if neither of these arrangements should seem satisfactory to you, I feel sure that members of the faculty would gladly entertain our guests in their own homes."

Miss Gorham was silent for a moment, but it seemed clear that she was really considering the possibilities mentioned. Finally she broke the silence by remarking, "I shall call a meeting of the committee soon and discuss with them the suggestions you have made and will write you later of our decision." She bade me good night as she held out her hand, not quite so stiffly, I dared think, as when she had first welcomed me, and I hurried back home.

At the first opportunity next day I sought out Mrs. Edward Harris, the wife of " Derwall " Harris's son, who had recently joined the Amherst faculty as assistant to his father in Chemistry. Both were young, and as the Harrises were next-door neighbors of ours, I had known Ned for many years and his wife for several. Furthermore, I knew that Mrs. Harris, like Mrs. Todd, was not afraid of innovations and was rightly considered a good sport. I told her of my interview and of my proposals and asked her advice. " Do you think," I queried, " that if Smith should accept the faculty home proposition that enough of the faculty wives would be interested to make the thing work? "

" I know this," she answered breezily, " I'll take care of as many as this flat will hold, provided your committee will supply the beds and bedding. Let's measure the place and see how much space we have."

We found a tape-measure and on our knees covered the several rooms. Our final reckoning was that if beds were placed close together we could put in twenty-one. " Count on us for twenty-one girls, if you have that many to spare," laughed this good friend, as I thanked her and hurried away. From the Harris flat in Hunt's Block I made my way to the Todds', where I repeated my story to Mrs. Todd. " Fine," was her opening comment. " I am sure that I can take from ten to twelve, though I may have to call on the committee for an extra bed or two." With these assurances I felt confident that we could put the thing over, provided, as I had been inclined to believe, the Smith authorities would chose this arrangement should they decide to let the girls stay at all. The news of our plan spread rapidly, and we were fairly deluged with requests from faculty wives to be counted in when assignments were made. Before the deluge ended we had only two or three girls each for Mrs. Harris and Mrs. Todd.

In the meantime we waited eagerly for the word from Smith that would decide our fate. It finally came in the form of an unexpectedly friendly note from Miss Gorham. The committee had decided, she wrote, that the young ladies might pass the night of the prom in Amherst with the understanding that they would be entertained in the homes of members of the faculty. And they were so entertained that year and for many years after until, indeed, faculties like parents succumbed to the influence of this mad and modern world and callously abandoned all semblance of control over the activities and whereabouts of their pupils outside of classroom hours.

Anyway, the Ninety-Four Junior Prom Committee felt, and still feels, that it made history for Amherst. I often wish that I had preserved that letter from the chairman of the Smith College Squelch Committee. It would deserve a high place in the Amherst memorabilia collection.

The Senior Prom of my junior year brought us face to face with a problem wholly new in Amherst's long history — the race issue. There were two outstanding Negroes in that class, William Lewis and William Jackson, both of whom had attained high distinction in scholarship, athletics, and public speaking. Both had played on the football team, and Lewis had been its captain. Jackson had made a record on the track team as well, and Lewis was his classmates' choice for class orator. And both were well liked by all. So far so good, but when it was announced that both these fellows had bought prom tickets and were preparing to bring partners of their own race and color, pandemonium broke loose. The college was in an uproar, and the student body was split wide open. So was the faculty. Nothing else was talked about, and as the time for the dance drew near, the line between the opposing sides was clearly drawn. A goodly number of the students turned back their tickets and noisily announced that they would not attend. Several of the faculty wives refused the customary invitations to serve as patronesses. Old friends, students and faculty alike, became enemies on this issue. Champions appeared on each side to lead and urge on their followers. Among the students, Charles D. Norton, later President Taft's private secretary, took the lead in behalf of the liberals. Norton was one of the most popular men in college, and his enthusiasm for the cause brought not a few wavering souls into the ranks. He personally took charge of the dance cards of his colored friends, tackling the most prominent fellows in the college, whom he vigorously urged to put their names down for dances with the partners of their Negro classmates and even to allow him to enter the names of these same classmates on the cards of their own lighter skinned partners. It was a hard struggle, but eventually he won out and the cards of both were filled.

Norton at the time was deeply interested in Miss Garrison of Smith, a granddaughter of the famous abolitionist, and his mates were convinced that she was the inspiring influence and guiding spirit in Norton's crusade. The fact that she later became his wife would seem to indicate that this conviction was not wholly wrong.

Between opposing faculty wives the gulf steadily widened, and the prom committee was hard put to it to fill out the list of patronesses. In the end they had to go outside the ranks of the regular candidates and even bring in some ladies from the town. I recall that my broad-minded mother gladly accepted such an invitation, though under ordinary circumstances she would have much preferred to remain at home.

The prom as scheduled was finally held, though the attendance was light. No untoward incident occurred to mar its progress. Those present enjoyed themselves thoroughly, but it was many months before tongues ceased to wag and friendly relations were again restored between those who had been so suddenly and unexpectedly separated when this puzzling issue confronted them.